*Heavenly Bodies ~
Celestial Alignments
Feeling ~ Energy that Is
LOVE in Itself*

Sunny Jetsun

<u>Dhammapada</u>
*'Hate does not dispel hate * only Love dispels hate'*

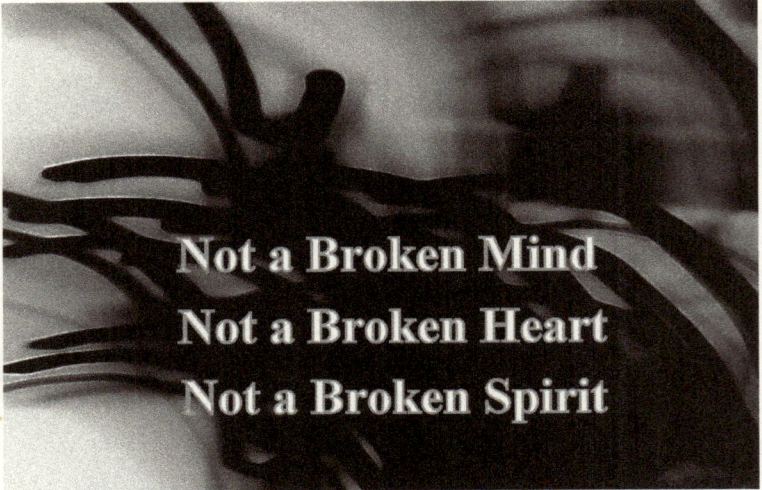

Not a Broken Mind
Not a Broken Heart
Not a Broken Spirit

Artwork by T Bird a pseudonym of Sunny Jetsun

All names, characters, and incidents portrayed in this book are fictitious. No identification with actual persons, is intended or should be inferred.

Heavenly Bodies ~ Celestial Alignments Feeling ~ Energy that Is LOVE in Itself

Sunny Jetsun

Books by the Same Author:

'Driving My Scooter through the Asteroid Field
Coming Down Over Venus ~ Hallo Baba'
**'Light love Angels from Heaven. New Generation,
Inspiration, Revolution, Revelation ~
All the Colours of Cosmic Rainbows'**
'Green Eve * Don't lose the Light Vortex *
My brain's gone on holiday ~ free flowing feelings'
**'Surfing or Suffering ~ together * Sense Consciousness
fields of a body with streams and stars of hearts'**
"When You're happy you got wings on your back ~
Reposez vos oreilles a Goa; We're only one kiss away"
'Psychic Psychedelic'
'Streaming Lemon Topaz Sunbeams'
'Invasion of Beauty *FLASH* The Love Mudras'
'Patchouli Showers ~ Tantric Temples'
'It's Just a Story ~ We Are All the Sun, Sweet Surrender'
Anthology #1 ~ 'Enjoy The Revolution'
Anthology # 2 ~ 'Love & Freedom ~ Welcome'
'He Lives In a Parallel Universe'
'Queen of Space ~ King of Flower Power ~ dripping Rainbows'
'All Love Frequency ~ In Zero Space'
*Peace Goddess*Spirit of the Field*The Intimacy Sutras*
'I've been to Venus & back*These Are Real Feelings*
Let the Universe Guide Your Heart*through Space'
The Kiss in Slaughterhouse 6

'It's better to have Loved
And Lost than to have never
Loved' That's Not true
because you can never lose!

My Heart Has Melted ~
You Are My Dream
Who are you?
You are my Oracle of Pure Emotion ~
Healing my Faded Aura.
You are my Overload of Blissful Senses.
My Erogenous Discoverer of Secret Zones.
My Breath ~ My Sustenance ~ My Fuel of Love.
You are the sweetest chickoo in my fruit salad.
My vanilla custard of Desire.
You are my Vision of Sincerity & Honour ~
with the Strongest hands to hold my heart ~
but soft enough to Soothe my Soul.
You are my Golden Key, my Happiness lottery.
You are my favourite cake.
My Divine chocolate bar with creamy skin to lick.
You are my pussy's Magician.
You are my Celestial Angel of Miraculous Orgasms.
My Humming Bird of Tantric pleasures ~
tasting my Sublime Nectar.
You are my Joy to Own & Share ~
Our Moments forever ingrained in a Myriad of Stars.
You are my Hope,
my Peace.
My only True, Open Hearted Lover.
You are my God of * Cosmic powers ~
My Light My Day My Night
You are the Keeper of my Seduction.
You are my Destiny
*

From 'Messages to the Lightworker'
By Surya Bliss

1

Bring in the Bees!

Prison feel ~ "I'm allowed to be here now Fuck Off!"
"Give me a chapati!" ~ As long as you stay in the matrix
conditioning, never be Free, kept as a cellular in solitary.
People hang on to demons, a race to the bottom of ethics!
Laughing, release, arranging the angles of reflection ~
Prism options, opinions, projecting ignorant reactions.
"Don't tell them God is dead!" ~ Experience perfection.
Resonating ~ How do you see the world, all other Life?
Afrikaans, "Bring back slavery, save a lot of problems"
'Boss Man' ~ Man who hits hardest; A clip is not a clap!
My own Intensity in the mirror ~ cycling of perceptions.
I end up with a knuckle in my mouth. ~ They should be
Shittin' themselves! Why? They own Mecca Avenue!
Walking down to Shiva Valley at a leisurely pace ~
'Enchantment of remoteness' ~ & Altruistic Robots!
Keep Loving regardless of this hologramic behavior.
'Time to celebrate life to infinity ~ and far beyond'
Nobody Inferior or Superior * just Is as (it) is ~
They don't want independent Tai Chi masters
turning up or any Qi Gong shared for Free!
Capturing a moment and letting it go ~
An instant to recheck meanings & values
"Ayuhuasca shows you what you need to see"
'Listening to the song of an endless river'
'Dreaming inside Vishnu's spiritual dream'
'THE WAR CAN BE OVER ANYTIME
IF WE ALL REALLY WANT IT TO BE'
She's a flat-out hippie * more High frequency ~

Laughing Yoga

Krishna stoned in his own Psychotropic Zone * Whitey off a chillum!
"Do you even really like me, if you don't what are you doing here?"
And if you do, show me! Dragging people to Paradise! Genuine,
Memory, Imagination, where is your Presence ~ in this moment,
the feeling of life in the body? Fields of Visual AWARENESS ~
nothing else left in the stillness. In the end you gotta love yourself.
Popular devotional art ~ Listening Stops Thinking.... In the now.

*

"Fuck Off!"-"You Fuck Off!"

We pick up ~ on others' energies ~ not living in time/timelessness.
'Firewood along Manikarnika Ghat, the smell of burning bodies ~
in the air ~ Reincarnation station, life and death meet in Varanasi'
That's your Consciousness and you're seeing ~ being aware of it!
It's not Personal, a Big illusion, a Giant Lie; No Humanity left.
Taken Conditioning to react like that!
Nature is the Ultimate, will push up ~
There's no end to anything!

*

Rambling Rose

Luscious, sleeping, dreaming, desiring, believing it's AWAKE!
Consciousness Expands ~ Open the curtain; Wake me up then!
<< 'ALWAYS BEING ON THE SUNNY SIDE OF LIFE' >>
Feeling, feeling the 'ME' reaction ~ The 'I AM' response.
There's no 'ME' no 'I' no 'Creation' no 'Enlightenment' ~
Not 'Real' ~ It's all coming from source of Cosmic Space.
Don't have to do anything ~ that's just how they are.
I Am the Divine ~ or you're stuck in 'ReACTION'
The 'Me' is in Unconscious Manifestation!
'I AM PURE CONSCIOUSNESS'

Poet of Light
"Your face is so blissfully serene when you are asleep"
"Yachting is on the house Baba ~"
Got everything they want in Chapora!
Don't you believe anything you hear about them!
Nowhere as peaceful as this ~ End of story.

*

Tending to be distracted under pressure!
"You put yourself where you blossom and grow or you die ~"
Tension will kill you, subjugated to stress & strain, body pain!
A Victim, Free of the consequences, living as a human being.
This moment ~ why spoil it with more anxiety attacks?
"All my pencils are lookin' at me ~ ha ha ha"
Pilgrimage just like Varanasi ~ 'Stuck in Goa!'
*"That makes sense to me*I get very disturbed*
if I don't have a smoke!"

*

Turn off the Mind ~ Turn on the Heart.
You may as well be on the other side of the World; Not here!
Then you know it's over! What's the point of me being there?
Turned off the Love; Stopped giving each other Ruby lips bliss.
See what happens ~ let it happen, finding its Level.
Sea snakes washed ashore on monsoon beaches ~
I was trying to be cool but it wouldn't Stop raining!
Completely uncomfortable, still mentally in the trip,
just want to be natural ~ all over the place at that time.
Where's the Off switch? Addicted to Love not its Obsession.
Shining out from all over your primal aura ~
*That's what I'm here for * Love's Connection*

Techno Smack * Machiavelli's Problem!
Ultimate motive, manipulation of/for Power.
'The Truth Is One' ~ 'One Is The Truth'
Being in Love ~ in the same frequency.
Taking away your fear ~ Afraid of the Fire.
He did all possible, then she said "Fuck Off!"
That's when he got it! Aware of being rejected.
Life after death an adventure into Nothingness.
Ready for Spaciousness * Cosmic Oceans of infinite Stars ~
Mind existence projecting ~ reflecting what, who you are now.
Fractal light Consciousness, lasers glowing in a crystal mirror.
Heavy stuff for the mind but not for you looking in the moment.
*
**

Remembering Flashbacks... "I Love You" (the best words)
Weeponised Biometric Drones, coming in hot, full of destruction!!!!
Chemical sensors, DNA analysis scan, legally blown to smithereens!
"I ran into that Mossad chick, Magnum in her hand at the 7.11"
"Picking up all the body parts darling!" "We'll go together."
"We lost the battle and lost Earth!" ~ Extrajudicial Assassinations...
Programmed to exterminate ourselves! "We gonna become extinct?"
Mushroom clouds on the horizon ~ They used Top secret chemicals!
"I think I'll move to Iceland ~ You know what I mean!"
From Off Planet ~ Security blasted them for their own Protection!
Memories all wiped clean; Remember what it was to have feelings?
Now fully rebooted with Information, mirages have no sense or truth.
"We're Not ET. Aliens we're Human!" "Do we have to let them die?"
Super ecstasy in Paradise ~ Dreaming of us in a Cosmic embrace!
"You're Not Who You Believe You Are" ~ on the Oblivion mission.
"Your Cosmicness is still in there somewhere!"

Funky * Ishtar

Rock up for a picnic ~ Reality is Artistic.
Highly suggestible to being Alpha waves.
We'll start to watch it and be brainwashed!
Face it, Daleks are pretty stupid too Master?
Dancin' like a maniac, where the f..k am I?
DMT. trip to telepathic dolphins and whales ~
Being chased by orbs of light for a few nights
with other non-human humans Off Planetary.*
He's left some vital evidence ~ Wisdom.
Raga ~ don't take anything too seriously.

*

Top Slave

"Who wants to move to Caracas, city of the most murders?"
'Cleaner the coke the better the crack!' King Demon said.
It'll shake you up a bit ~ I hope I don't get Dementia..
Being Aware I'm observing this Theatre of Consciousness.
'There's a utopian lining to every rainbow sprinkling cloud'
A cool wound, those endorphins must mean something!
Like the Realisation of a dream; I am Cosmic Source self.
Transmutable ~ Love is Freedom ~ allowing it all to be ~

*

Immune Systematic

Love & Happiness ~ can't get better than that!
The Knower not having to Prove who you are!
Feeling your Presence ~ Is what you are,
*your attention on your breath ~ Inner*Self*
because ~ I'm listening without mental activity...
*Where your Awareness goes * that's where it's at.*

Divineloving@wetnet

Negate Suffering ~ "This is what you did to me!"
Slap, slap, slap, smack, kick in the groin, knee in
solar plexus, pulled my broken arm, stood on me!
Here comes the blame transfigure to a flame again!
Everything leaves you one way or another ~
If you don't leave it, it leaves you; Ask Anatta.
Just the Idea of it ~ You simply see the lights...
As one heart of Love ~ revolving in the Cosmos.

*

FULL SPACESHIP

"You give and take what you need"
The Crystal lights up the room ~
Penetrating into a sparkling pool.

*

DIVINE LOVE

'To see the ONE in all you see'
"Who wants Heaven on Earth?"
Dazzling green stars in her oniric eyes
twinkling in cascading ~ luscious hair.
"I am the dreamer you are the dream"
LIFE* LOVE* LIGHT* SPACE

*

Real Freedom Gene

I have come for a glorious memory ~ but it's gone.
Changing each moment ~ being together in bliss.
"Cum on me" cum to me ~ 'Manage your Craving!'
The smile in your eyes tells me everything about ~
lights inside you ~ All part of Bhakti * Cosmic truth.

Hearts full of Vulvas!
You bring a candle into a dark place…
"The Demon of this chakra is Attachment"
You need a destination, a star to follow ~
Not wandering lost, parched in an endless desert.
"There's not even any branches, how did I get up here?"
'She died on the way to hospital, she was very happy;
She'd saved her children!'

*

Turmeric Gels
Legs akimbo ~ 'Head up their own Ass Asana'
Their addiction to Thinking ~ Ego try a mudra.
Clearing the source of inflammation ~
"You have to use two hands & mouth"
"That is a fuckin' Robot Baba!"
Betrayed in a Cosmic way.

*

No Slave * No Master!
"Thank you we're gonna take a break, the cops are here."
'No touching, no photos!' My name is Sperm Avatar ~
Freedom is Courage! You are always Free to respond!
"If you don't control your mind, someone else will"
Freedom is there in any given situation ~
Our behaviour is conditioning * of our genes.
You are Ego within the Phenomenal Theatre.
He answers to his name, the Sage knows it.
He's not the doer ~ the natural puppeteer.
You think it's the reflection in the mirror ~
"We are Devils, you are Slaves." "I'm not!"

Shack Incognito

Here you can really feel the inside space ~
Looking outside into a sunlit jungle garden
Light gleaming beautifully everywhere ~
Immediate awareness of these two hemispheres!
Sense of realisation, nature in my happy heart.
Knowing

*

Bones in a Wetsuit.

"I wouldn't want to be eaten by a Crocodile"
Doesn't really matter if you're dead!
'LIVE & LET DIE'
"Let the dead bury the dead"
It's not your problem let 'em get on with it.
They don't want to work, dumping it on you.
Seven guilders the bounty on a Jewish head!
Your Inability to Integrate with the new society coming!
'Just agree to be different' ~ underneath the problem.
"We're sharing a similar field of ULTRA * sensitivity"
'Don't need the Fear' altho' encourages COURAGE.
Using it to understand the human condition….
Anger inducing you to change ~
"Everyone's talkin' 'bout Uruguay!"
Fuels of Inspiration * love & Peace.

*

Acupuncture * CosmicMagnets.com

"I'll stab you in the face!"
"Thank you ~ how much?"
"Acid is very Spiritual"

Old wine in new soft skin
How old are you? Your Akashi Soul!
Always fresh flowers coming up ~
The Knower witnessing the Beautitudes.
"Be grateful, be thankful or you become a
Shithead, Yeah man!" Step back, wake up!
Shamans dropping keys all the time ~
to get you out of your virtual Prison!
Keys to the Kingdom of Heaven...
Respecting the Magic of all Life.
*

Revolutionary Yoga
You smoke pot and "I was tripping on the sky"
Sniff, sniff ~ plants screaming when pulled up!
Snakes weaving together connecting all nature ~ beautiful!
"I don't think Enlightenment is based on Suffering or Torture"
Zen there is No one ~ Getting my head around it with a 'Response'
Now your own river is starting to flow ~
Pouring out ~ shooting through the wild rapids.
Guided to your attributes, letting Opinions go ~
Latent self is growing up, not a struggle anymore!
In clarity is Epiphany.
*

Going Into Being ~ Singularity
*I AM * I AM CONSCIOUS * I LIKE IT ~*
Trying to teach Integrity not a full Mind Massage!
*Tao stars still twinkle * Zen stones are the smoothest.*
It's already done ~ Past, present, future all FORMATION.
Virtual games of 3 dimensional manifestation, duality for us
*to see * to feel the Synchronicity ~ happening, becoming.*

<u>Without Lead</u>
Pointless sharing your time with Mind invaders.
He hypnotised them into loving him; she did the same mate.
Just do the right thing, doesn't matter if you get killed for it.
"When I was in there never felt like being locked up"
Holding up the light of Integrity ~
Throwing their people into the fire.

*

<u>Smart people running the World!</u>
"We all run the World" ~ taking different positionings.
"Someone's gotta lead these folks to salvation, Hari Krishna"
Iran hangs gay kids out on the street! "We moved on from
Public executions, ain't we? Who is this Great Satan?
Heads on Pikes! "I'm a free man I don't fit in any box"
Things come and go ~ people at different stages of self.
No it's life ~ it's horrendous; Rwanda Tutsi, 'Chop chop!'
Buddhists being chilled, compassion reality, consciously
not taking its free-will away, part of the natural, normal life.
Not enough Tiger Balm left, the others are only surviving ~
they don't have any empathy for those slaughtered animals.
The silent whimpering of the pigs! ~ I needed to see that!
You find your heart then.

*

<u>Auto Happy End</u>
"Thought I wanted a boyfriend" ~ Only really wanting
a front loading washing machine, with a tumble Action.
Fuzzy Wobble ~ options for an extended cycle function.
Pressing Sari Settings ~ rinsing with full spin satisfaction!

Ruling the Unruly by La Guillotine!
Beating up people for protesting against Fracking nature!
Aren't Governments supposed to represent the people?
It's Cosa Nostra, NSA; Their National Interest & Security!
Be H A P P Y regardless ~ It's inside you forever & ever.
Crushing YOUR skull, purifying through their T E R R O R.
A Vatican patent, 'Punishment Machine' severe trauma tool.
Did you find the 'Pear of Anguish' ~ Inserting it into a vagina?
Designed for unholy women accused of blasphemy, adultery,
Prostitution; Called her heretic, working for her master Satan!
The Pape blessing you with more excruciating P A I N!
They'll continue to Control your Life if you let them ~
*S H I V A * I S * T H E U L T I M A T E * P A G A N*

*

Planet Shukra
Hey next time you're in England visit the 'AntiChrist'
Everything you read in a Hamburg magazine come true!
Bunnies on Tap at the Sihanoukville's Happy End House.
"You don't force your imagination onto anyone"
Hardcore ~ "I'm dying for a chillum and a coffee!"
With £1 million in the bank you don't need cosmetic surgery.
"I was beaten by my drunken husband so you can stick it out too!"
There's no escape, beating you up, leaving home in a hearse ~
after satisfying them in the kitchen & bedroom ~ That's your job!
Did you smirk at me because you saw me naked on the beach?
She cracks a skull with hammer & nail, I'm nervous eating cow.
I lost my total determination and you got a smile on your face.
"We're not raping you out of sexual lust but to teach you
a lesson not to be out alone after sunset" ~ Salaam.

Thedangerousdrugcompany.com
Celtic Irish Magic, get off the Stage, you're too hot on!
A holy relic, one hair of Mohammed has been found to be missing ~
from a village shrine, is recovered; The state had gone into mourning.
Recognising the plight of how many people living in the world today.
"Full torture you find your heart or not!" Positive Mother Earth.
Memory inhibitor, pain killer, definitely having some of that!
Consciousness at rest ~ becoming Conscious, sleeping 'Me'
barefoot magic ~ Awareness 'I'

*

Pain of the Body
"It's horrible to see people suffering ~
That's not true; Suffering is a Choice
It's only reaction of the Mind"
Totally responding to Life,
having no meaning to life!
Brothers & sisters fanning each other ~
little fluffy clouds; We Are Stardust essence
Sugar's* sweetness ~ two things you can't separate.
I * Me.

*

'Let the dead bury the dead' ~ Awakening!
Why cause suffering to anyone? ~ So straight forward!
Obvious that it's insane but people believe it's truly Real.
Against the National Psyche ~ making it into 'Democracy'
OK put a label on it, why not? But won't for GMO products!
What you got to hide, what is our Gov. allowing you to hide?
For whose benefit is all this unnatural, inhumane, toxic stuff?
Need a Psychedelic walkabout ~ 'Trips I have Known & Loved'

13

Passion Vale

Peaceful, Conscientious Objector; Enjoying a cognac ~
with an attractive blonde who wants to be alone with you.
Escaping to the mountains, we like to play with shadows.
You're a Scorpio mystery, gotta maintain them Trance!
There's your axe go out there and kill something!
Spear in your groin ~ a death on the battlefield.
Full of Kali's dead bodies ~ a hole like Hell!
Angel of mercy coming to take you to Heaven.
You're in shock, the light comes, you let it go.

*

Who Owns What!

HNII; 'Capitalist Jesuits own the Bank of America; Surprise!
IRS tax dollars are deposited in the Virtual Vatican Treasury!'
Piercing the Corporate veil, following the classical money trail.
Ask the Oracle who owes $17 trillion to International financiers?
"If this is it I can't do it anymore!"

*

Time to Dance

"We're squatting your place, we'll get out for a grand!"
Lookin' at new expressions all the time ~ shared by a
pod of Amazonian pink dolphins ~ in it for the pleasure!
Affinity together ~ Ask the baleine whisperer for a hot tip.
DNA ~ not just local but from the other side of the world.
From beyond the Van Allen belt, to other infinite Universes.
Here they still murder heretics & decapitating women, alone,
driving in the wrong lane without any license for their brain!
You never know when the Ruling dynasty will fuck you up again!
*CELEBRATE, forget the Conceptualisation ~ B E * H A P P Y*

Pure chemical enhancement
"He would have loved it for what it was"
Raw Chocolate Protects Your Brain....
You go to Holy places you find Charas ~
Comin' from a party a little bit wasted.
Hallucinogenic Punch a Birthday treat.
Barefoot dancing around in the Sun.
"I'd love to do that"
*

Parable of Animal Farm
What more story of reality do you need than that?
KEEP IT SIMPLE ~ Why fix it if it ain't broke mate?
Sound bites, signals changing our attention frequency.
Light blue fishnets, "I thought I was at the Thai Meridian!"
Quantum makes everything happen all of a sudden!
"Don't hold the budgie too tight or you'll kill it!"
"When you have a nation of simple, naive sheep
you have a Government of rapacious wolves"
Temple Taxes & fines, perpetuating themselves.
Does God approve of Online Gambling, Pape?
Depends on which Infidel God is in Power!
Always the pigs who assume the top position
then corrupted for the sake of their own interests.
What is the Salvation Vision of the future if any?
NSA. is inside your Holographic, nanomind now!
Confused by the constant paranoid brainwashing!
Built on the War Machine, military complex profiting evil.
Open up the Power of Love.

Raising the Vibes of our Planet
****

Shown a Miracle made by a Siddhi.
What enlightenment? Forget it all.
Even the elements will obey you!
The Universe ~ cannot deny it.

*

Aligning Our Thoughts
When we are high vibration ~ we are the light. "Renoir's my
favourite artist, hers was Rolf Harris, by Royal appointment."
"The King's court is so wicked with their Jimmie Saville tattoos
it's really taking the Piss mate!" Look, wake up to that bullshit!
A clip on the head, Government production then go and die.
Did you feel the Maharajah's elephant crushing your skull?
"I'm not in the Bedouin dimension ~ He'll stone his daughter
in the desert, I can't talk to him!" Everybody wants WMD;
You bomb me I'll Bomb you more; We're all made Insane!
Coming from a party with Shagger Baba a little bit wasted!
Better to not have a broken leg than to have a broken leg ~
Kicking the Gecko to see if it was alive! Shit happens, Yeah!

*

Fantastic * Reality
Barefoot jumping around in the uncensored Sun.
There's something lovely about butterflies today ~
Its boundless, raw, naked, Unconditional Love for all.
Resonating ~ just enjoy each and every moment please.
Not making things complicated, complex projections ~
"Snow's comin' on Sunday" ~ "Is there anything to read?"
Old enough to get a tattoo, young enough to be pierced!

16

<u>Lights on no one's home!</u>
Depends on your aim in the Universe * Being happy suffering ~
If you don't want pleasure & pain, doesn't bring you happiness!
"Animals are humans, it doesn't have to be like this in the factory!"
"Women are up in the air, disengaged, space chaos needs Form control"
Men are on top of the food chain ~ 'Hunters, gatherers, providers'
'Let's all sing the 'Reggae Marseillaise'
"And they even nicked his stablisers"

*

<u>Bottle of Mushroom Tea</u>
'CometoGoatosleepwithwhitewomen.com'
It's what we'd call Sexual harassment!
Moths attracted by the light ~
We need a few good Omens!
"My purpose in Life is to be happy
loving my spirit, you sweetheart and Mother Earth."
"I married a Sadhu and lived in a Himalayan cave!"
"I don't wanna go anywhere where they're gonna cut my
throat, decapitate me with a trowel & eat my eyeballs!"
Orgy ~ the taking of too much!

*

<u>Naked Meditation</u>
"Why work when you can sit around all day and do nothing ~?"
Organic raw chocolate protects your brain from any nervous
degenerating disease ~ and it'll bring your memory back! What?
Nobody likes a smart arse, everybody loves a great pair of tits!
Full visual the whole place is an animated scene.
No straight edges ~ all waves *** 'Stepping over Galaxies'
Channeling Acid into lots of crystal drops!

Ultimate*Intimate

Honouring Sita ~Thanks to women's Bhakti Goddess.
Why're Indian men so obsessed with their f... cricket?
Extremely frustrated, harshly teasing Eve's Sati sari!
Raped her, put her in the blazing flames, new rituals ~
old rites, Ignorance! Part of my becoming ~ Intuitive.
No one owns anything not even your good old name,
or my Ganesh Biddhis, a Maharaja's feudal privilege!

*

Psyche Porn

Want a license to Fuck your brains out?
It ain't my Job to make people happy!
I am who I am ~ 'Quack Quack Quack'
'Inhale ~ change ~ die' ~ transmitting ~
"I can see the lines, furrows in your heart"
They show you glittering and you follow it,
puts a smile on your face ~ for a moment.
'If you enjoy it be happy'

*

Typhoon's Plastic Smoke Bubble Bath

From now Bangladesh is closed, no more sweatshop goods!
She has telepathic lovers ~ felt them in her dreams last night.
'Package to Goa is when you know how good it is in Lanzarote;
Nice having white sheets, no rats, cockroaches, rubbish & filth!'
We're the servants of God on sanitation, Hygiene & recycling.
It's not about other's attitudes, it's about You fallen Angel.
Not more sense but more destructive capabilities!!!
'Oceans of Information ~ not a drop of wisdom'
Just enough I'm done, 'Hare Ram'

<u>Wake 'em up!</u>
That's Christ living inside us ~
"I was talkin' to Jesus the other day"
"Where do you live?" "In the hearts of people."
Thought is the enemy ~ the river that takes you
You have to know what you want and don't want.
"It's a lovely Planet ~ It's our home"
Real is Real.

*

<u>Really taking the Piss!</u>
Doesn't matter what anyone says, none of it is absolutely Real!
Ed Snowden should get a Noble Peace Prize, Obama won it!
Monsanto winning most Ignoble GMO. Prize for Agriculture.
Outrageous who the F.... do they think they are?
"We're not here to judge anyway!"
"Innocence is in your own head ~"
"There is the Magic of the Lingham"
Smoking a spliff because you enjoy it.
Programmed for reactions ~ Attitude!

*

<u>Maharaja Muppet</u>
Creating the World as we go ~ none of it is true.
"I wanna be Free" ~ "You're always Free"
Projecting your own Identity onto the World.
It's You who can do it all ~ It's up to You.
Say it's about lifestyle at the end of the day.
Just being aware of sitting here ~ 'Wei Wu Wei'
Everything's remotely automatic... Try that one!

Hot Gun finger on her trigger.
Crack pipes smoking during Russian sunsets.
"Nazi bitch." "Come on she had a name once!"
We carry each other's Karma ask Madame Kali Skaya.
Viagra's for Pussies ~ "Fucking me right here & now!"
"I feel the Ecstasy don't have to define it just feel it"
The point of having some FUN.
You got the rock and roll in you.

*

No dialogue ~ he's dead!
You're having a battle in your head ~
Then don't have any opinion, not even
that, that Giant Redwood is just a 'Tree!'
*In stillness, silence * I Am * Cosmically ~*
You find the things you need from nature.
What do you feel you need each morning?
"We're dreaming thinking we're awake"
Full of the river ~ he's raising the dead!
It seemed to come together by itself.
"Burn the thing when you're done!"

*

Who, what, when, where, how?
Doesn't matter as long as you're there ~
Not a waste of courage; freedom is Unity.
You get in touch with your own Master.
S/he's talkin' to you; I try not to Stop it.
"It's hard living in a Christian family"
All that Fear ~ the dogs like the Reiki.
It's my Karma to be who I am.
'Your Truth is Your Truth'

HEARTLESS OCTAVE

You sound like a spoilt brat & ……..
"Some people are born with a high Love vibration"
"If you live in the moment and are happy Now
why stop to be happy somewhere else?"
Energy resonating at Love's higher frequency ~
Attracted to you, your being ~ Living in Love vibration space.
Energy vibrating all our chakras, expressing Divine qualities.
Love raising us to a state of highest consciousness ~
all that is inspiring, empowering, enhancing Life.

*

Rattlin' her all night

No Speed dating necessary * No Oxygenator.
A tablet to make you feel ~ being in touch.
Don't feel bad in the morning come down.
Her eyes are hangin' out like this and ~
he tells you what he did to her last night!
Sitting on the dance floor with a bag of MDMA.
He loves his drugs, he loves his women and his 100 mg. Cialis!
"More Power comes from saying No" ~ someone once said, why?

*

The Lazy Stripper

"Mothers are ok but not the girlfriends!"
Super proud with two big thick dicks.
Never satisfied ~ Sweet sadness,
She lives in my heart.
You don't need saving! "It's clarity, no more ME"
The energy's the same, the person is different.
An Ashram just happens ~ of its own accord.

A Magical Job
It gives you something back ~
Doing it with all of your heart.
Full of Love ~ fall in Love and magnetic devotion.
Raising our vibrations ~ In tune with her Venus' full moon.
Anjuna freaks, Arambol hippies, Yoni-Yoginis, slips of the tongue.
"It's very hard to let go ~ to let go of what you really Love!"
All that trust, intimacy, desires, auras & deepest memories.
"If you feel Love, that's all you want"
"Loving you is over ~ long live Love"
"Unconditional Love is all over too"
Love energy chakra * Open feelings
*

Luscious Heart Id
She's lost our full power Loving feeling ~
and doesn't seem to want to get it back at all.
Get your head around that one reality Baby!
It's all about My Mind! Feeling ~ Absolutely.
My frequency still desiring your frequency ~
My dopamine entwined in your crystalline
body not to mention your gorgeous vagine.
Smelling lovely in her Pink wet sunshine.
What are you waiting for?
*

It has a Program
There's no one there to be home ~
Can't Control your own environment.....
"You can only truly love when you are naked"
When you are Not afraid ~
Bliss is in * vulnerability

Happy little Gaia electrons.

Rainbow Honey, Anjuna beach commercially exploited;
Anti hippy, anti social, fear and loathing in Goa today!
Dying for a chillum and a coffee at Bom Shanti's shack.
Understanding looking into your eyes to communicate.
"I can honestly say I never joined the corrupt rat race"
Banksters kicking your assets and no justice to boot!
They're going to make it illegal to grow your own seeds…
Try some Aquaponics, hydroponics, permaculture its real.

*

Guilty as Sin!

Getting their own back once ~ overcome by anger...
They need help, they've gone mad, it's fuckin' horrible!
Everyone needs help here but they need it much more!
Wake up everybody don't be such serious Elves & Pixies.
Feelings in the mind * feelings in the heart ~ "I Love You"
Coming with the feeling rather than thinking about it too much.
You're at ease, you're at peace; She's free to be herself.
Surrendering essences of it in a very natural way.
Free Love ~ Living it in the supra * spiritual way.

*

Wonderland Thighland

We're from different Planets 'Junoon Bhakti' not land of fake smiles!
Just being in the moment ~ when we are together; 'Sawadee Krap'
Her hormones are provoked by a lot of misunderstanding.
Zap it off, sniff it, 'click here if you are Toxic', Dab it off!
Mental angels on diamond crystals healing the addiction
to thinking, transmuting the obsessional, mental-movement
of smoking a cigarette ~ sent outside in the freezing rain!

Dead Whales Glowing In the Dark

The Sea is boiling at the Fukushima plant, Japan; Poisoned Planet!
(300 tons of highly radioactive water discharged each day into the
sea over 3 years. Radioactive element Plutonium's got a shelf life
of 240,000 years, one of most potent carcinogens. 20-40 trillion
Becquerels of Tritium into the Pacific ~ Downplayed by the scientists!
What's the likelihood that radiation will spread a Global catastrophe?
Strontium 90 is poisonous for 300 years; China Syndrome's arrived!
Inducing Mutations ~ food chain continuously irradiating y/our cells!
Heavily radiated rods sitting in a bath on the roof cooling off!
Going up like a time-Bomb anytime ~ Mushroom clouds Ahoy!
You can see smoke, can't see radiation at Paradise Beach, CA!
Not a Geiger counter in sight, there has to be a reason for that!
Dreaming of a white Xmas * Radioactive snow falling in Missouri!
*
SAVING US FROM A WAR.

Sitting in a Circle chanting Love & Compassion ~
& on the street too. You have to say you don't F.... like it!
We'll let you out of prison but you gotta keep to our Conditioning.
Those of spreading greed, hate, fear, slavery, full on exploitation!
People are living immersed in nature, we need to protect this life.
They've no idea what a TV or Gas, Tesco or Darkpsy is; No idea!
What're we teaching young kids? Displaying of stuffed Reindeer.
Getting different downloads, programs, culture from off Planet X.
Looking at a forlorn foetus in a jar next to the spices and herbs.
"When I had that brain in my hands ~ F... it's a human being!"
Gave me a CD of my eye operation. "I've been under the Knife!"
Impersonally * Objective ~ "Never again will I cut up a snail."

Wanting to Live in Paradise.

Do mining conglomerations have any rationalist link to Gorillas?
'She shouldn't have called Africans animals as she loved animals!'
Feeding genetic strangers, transcend electronic brain programming!
All to survive proceed in our quest, destiny through the Cosmic gates.
Where is Your Free will ~ with or without genes he topped himself!
Logic of the onboard computer for passing on your karmic codes ~
Who's desirous for all minerals and treasure on Earth at any cost?

*

Supra Eugenic Holograph

*'Think World Without Girl Children' * STOP this practice Right Now!*
A policy of Divide and Rule programmed into their genes' instinct.
Natural selection inside a slaughterhouse along Rwandan streets.
Not extreme ~ I want to survive and continue on my Cosmic destiny.
They could change the whole World right now with 4 phone calls!
Met a naked Sadhu "why should I meet the king, tell him to come
here & meet me in the jungle!" Wealth controls the common man!
He sent him a thousand slave girls dripping in gorgeous jewels.
"I have no attachments ~ I have renounced all Worldly things"
"I have nothing but you have the World ~ of Ego attachment to lose!"
"We've given him enough respect now bring that Naga Baba in chains!"
'Money the Ultimate Maya' ~ The Emperor placed his hands outside
his coffin showing he could take nothing material into the afterlife ~
He'd killed so many in many wars of suffering; What did it achieve?
The wrong rape festival! Ethnic cleansing, the Messenger of Death!
Can't take a blade of grass with you even from the Tantric Ashram.
Apparently all the Plankton is dying in the Pacific ~ Save our Planet!
"Buy a hammock, family size ~ I was pulling the natural FUN card"
Beauties beyond the human imagination, can you feel that?

<u>Best Dreams When Awake * In tune ~ Intuitive</u>
Big Smile ~ that's what's important! Freedom to get off your head!
"I like people HAPPY" ~ You know what's comin' next!
Ultimately having a laugh is good not an Astral Rejection in the arse!
*Bhagvata Purana inspiration * her eyes resembling Lotus flowers ~*
His chest was marked with the lines of the Goddess of Fortune.
She did it one night.

*

<u>Enjoyment Design</u>
Happiness comes in small doses! STDelights.
They exist differently in different places ~
You can virtually proposition any of them!
Hugging me all the time ~ I had to say "behave!"
Shocked, even the nice girls are thinking about it...
Shakti sisters shakin' their arse! It used to be a Pussy Palace.
Wrapped us up in the cocoon of Lust .

*

<u>WE ARE THE UNIVERSE</u>
"Corruption is from the grass roots level all the way to the stars!"
"You are not a human being you are an Inter*dimensional being
having human experiences" Consciousness in its Purest Form.
Interactions of your Aura burning the flame of all your Senses!
Natural vibration, sounds, mantras, Universe is flowing energy!
Shiva dancing in the membrane of the Cosmos through eternity.
Spirit, matter, dualities, polarities; Now it seems all One ~"YES!"
Seeing Sacred Temples in the Forest ~ "Life Itself Is Spiritual"
Controlled by silly thoughts; The bottom line ~ Is feeling GOOD.
'Those dirty cunts, that ignorant twat, he's a wanker, she's a dike,
they're activists, they're Infidels, she's a slag and it's a f.... Alien!'
There's No *ME* all just a fantastic illusion then it becomes clear.

Extinction (Oxfam)

'World's 85 richest have same wealth as poorest 3.5 billion'
'Music is art from the Heart' ~ transmitting sound waves.
Killing the last Black Rhino to make snuff from its horn!
Plug in to it, headphones, listening to Satanic frequencies...
Who the f... is watching this stuff, Monster in front of your face?
Addicted, anti-social kids going around smashing up things!
Bullshit off the scale, Primal Malice in Wonderland Sheriff!
Being a slave and not having a clue that we are f.... slaves!
The rampant Corporate symbology of a 'New World Order'
This is bigger than McDonald's ~ 'I'm Loving It' or Coca Cola!
Gone through the Pillars of Isis feeding the Beast dark energy.
All 'Yes Men' to 'PR. Programs' hidden by Global Puppeteers.
Won't tell where the Gold is; wants you online, RFI. or tracking
you down the street! I'm still on a Cosmic voyage of discovery.

***

FREE SOLAR POWER ~ OMNIFISCENT ENERGY**
It's all about Availability ~ Make the most of it while we can!
India ~ "Why get married in the first place?" Locked in a box.
That Monkey Mind, 'If you can Stop Thinking, You Remember'
Organic Mate; "Giving to the children the most important thing
how to look after their own kids." A Procreative Global Vision ~
Frequency into a new dimension * new frequency ~ ad infinitum.
Creating matter from light as Shamanic Sufis dancing by a fire.
We'll have to give them a lot of MDMA. before the Revolution!
"The only way to defeat the System Is to swallow it whole"
Please do something with it that makes common sense ~
Every life Form treated with equal respect and value.
Giving Mother Earth a Gift.

Shakti In Every Direction!

She's manifesting her Maya ~ going where it's happening.
Something long & green & the girl with red in her golden hair.
You have to be honest about it ~ you're here to be a Pollinator!
The Devil's here to corrupt your intelligence, drinking your soul!
Sheeple being led by a Pied piper, I'll open my wings and fly!
Jellyfish swim with the flow ~ You flowing Multi*Dimensionally.
My heart is saying, 'I need a Preity Angel' ~ She'll do it for me.
16,000 Goddess wives & satisfying them all simultaneously!
Space is the boss for Courier frequencies ~ Cosmic healing
Trip on twinkling Shooting Stars*Left to receive*Right to give.
'Unity is Diversity' ~ "I Love all the pleasures I receive."

*

Spoken & Written ~ Nisargadatta Maharaj.

'Words, heard or read, will only create images in your mind
but you are not a mental image, you are the power of
perception and action behind and beyond the image.'
Spiritual Paradox, that you have to give up everything
to attain everything or what little bits you can do ~
Believe it or not ~ in the meantime be happy and smile

*

The Guardian: 'Alan Turing the second world war code breaker
who took his own life after undergoing 'chemical castration' following
a conviction for homosexual activity has been granted a posthumous
pardon 59 years after his death. A brilliant mathematician who played a
major role in breaking the Enigma code which arguably shortened WW11
by at least 2 years was pardoned under a Royal Prerogative of mercy by
the Queen following a request by the Justice secretary He was convicted
of gross indecency in 1952, admitting sexual relations with a man.'

& Didn't like the answer

"If you're not there to share it together what's the point darling ~?"
My head feels as a shrunken skull 'cause she was misconstrued.
Drilling my brain through the night so you can't take anymore!
'Out of sight out of mind' ~ Have to break it, use the pain!
Talkin' to himself. "I hit the floor like a ton of bricks!"
And I thought 'this is the End, the very last time!'
"Let's see what the Universe throws out"
Lost down that moist, pink rabbit hole.

*

VORTEX*ESSENCE

Why bother to go to Portugal when you're living in Phnom Penh ~
by the riverside or Sihanoukville beside green, crystal clear seas?
Coming out of a shoebox or bomb crater in the middle of the road,
walking around the Killing Fields ~ with your arms & legs missing!
They came from a tribe of Mindless Zombies, desensitised Drones
with the War ordinance Mind-boxset made for Demonic Genocide.
Turned out to be useless pissheads or crackheads with jackknives.
Country's run by an Oligarchy making people poorer and dumber.
Our miners were vilified for wanting to defend their livelihoods!
Spirit in their Heart ~

*

Cosmic Dyspraxia

You can drive yourself MAD thinking of things in the wrong way.
He might be a Scientologist but he might be into other things too.
His career is guaranteed just following his Manchurian Program.
They got it all back to front ~ It's about Giving all from the heart!
Happy day ~ sunbeams moving around at night beside Jade seas.
You gotta make people feel Welcome ~ being Engaged to a smile.

29

Sanitized

Bunch of Royal freeloaders on board; Playing around with Reality!
Unbelievable history of the World, it's not what they told me on TV.
I'm an off-planet Alienated Alien ~ Support your Truth Constitution.
What did you say about an Independent Greenback Mr. President?
It's almost Satanic programming, breathing in Chemtrail nanobots.
Where's all the Gold? That's what goes out first. Never on the News.
I have Dr. Death here, the thing cleansing this part of the Universe!
'You never see any Flying Saucer paintings at the Tate Modern!'
Coming to a house defies nature, we should be sitting on a leaf ~
They never say join the Army and Die, get a bullet in your head
but Join the Army become a man! Government Psychological Op.
Warfare on us! Came in right under the Radar & mesmerized me.
Power of the Voice ~ Auto suggestion, "Give me this, take that!"
Being Bombarded by brainwashing, propaganda and X Factor.
Traumatised; Keys to the back of your head ~ your personality.
With y/our arrogance we know nothing! Undermining the Truth.
Believing Sciences! Bending the rules in front of the spy cameras.
Tuning up synchronicity ~ try resonating deeper on a natural level.
Emphasising the sound of sacred*Psychedelic trance frequencies.
The vibrations of Authority or of Angels?

*

Goa Pills

"Send a drone round to the house!" Powers to Coerce, Control.
'We'll compensate you when she's confirmed as officially dead!'
"Darth Vader controls outer space ~ Yoda controls inner space"
Eaten a lot of Space cakes, high on chillums, wine & Sunshine.
Feeling good, settled, one with the couch ~ 'Go for a crazy one!'
You've been brainwashed all your life Dave, wake the fuck up!
They're pulling Dolphins out the sea ~ Massacred, piked to death!
You can push any button you want. 'I'm sick of shouting WANKER!'

Pharaoh * Moon * Frequency
Wild, absolutely volatile * smelling each other's musky scent ~
Female moths attract males over large distances even on stormy
nights, in conditions in which not even an owl would venture out.
Large antennae sense her sex molecules * starts his Flutter dance.
Once she is found and mates * fertilises ~ lays her eggs she dies.
Try some Bhang balls from the Government Pure Bombykol shop.
We have to tune into the Universe ~ meditating at Omkareshwar.
I had to remember how to breathe, attracting female silkworms!
She left a trail that I could follow to Paradise beach
*

A couple of girls on the go
"He's got everything around him that he likes ~"
I couldn't believe it, wasn't even lookin' when it happened!
You just wanna have FUN Baba ~ ABSOLUTELY
You're not a Slave; ABSOLUTELY, I've done that!
They're fiery little fuckers! This is laughing your head off FUN!
Stuck in the Paris; hot rain ~ her body was poetry in motion.
Taken straight to Stardom ~ singing it like the Ocean.
*

Meditation Rhythms
Combined Mind ~ Combined Energy.
Together it works * not in any conflict.
Demonic Negative mind; You don't know what Madness is!
Where are thoughts comin' from? They're there, you must decide.
What are you turning into ~ Illusions, actions, making a character!
That's You, y/our World, conditioned existence, sense of Realistic..
Watching your thoughts from the start, always come from the heart.
If you Watch your thoughts you'll see the intrinsic spaces ~
between the thoughts and won't get trapped by the thoughts.

<u>Enjoy where you are happy</u>
There is no change in 10 secs; 10 mins. or 10 hrs. ~
That's projecting into the future ~ doesn't seem real.
"I never see a barrier anyway it's only in the moment"
Turning up and the music's Psychedelic ~ being in tune!
Nice to have something that stills the Mind.
'Dali city it's got the cleanest air in China'
No Confucioness at the Potala Palace!

*

<u>Myam Myam</u>
Animals have souls of Unconditional love, 'woof ~ Bow, wow, wow'
He's so dependent he can't cook an egg or make a Tuna sandwich!
Dropped in the middle of a plastic sea ~ Nuclear core meltdown!!!
Saw only one Angel fish ~ We're all Cosmic; Can't neglect it Baba!
"I'll never be with a guy who has a snake in his house!"
It's not fair, a bull in severe trauma, blinded, shedding tears…
"They're primitive with a Neanderthal, violent mind-set, 21st C"
We got nicer people in Goa not that Taliban, they just don't get it!
'The lost tribe' ~ 'When in Anjuna have a smoke with a hippy Tour'
Witness miracles or You can leave your house & get hit by a spear!
Invisible Spirals we can't see are there, telepathic Quantum trance.
Sunshine's Circuit Board of crystal gems ~ Acoustic Resonation
Keep in your own Healing ~ full power entheogen, Energetic field.
All Planetary sequences ~ Aligning, tuning into a Galactic Vortex.
Radioactive plumes are circumnavigating our Planet every 40 days.
Aristotle split the World in two ~ Duality is coming from this untruth.
Man & God, me, you ~ Heraclites said 'whatever you say is not true'
What you say will become true ~ Everything is true, not true, truly.
It's All True ~ depends on who you're with in the here and now

Ultimate Pleasure

"The girl bends over so you can penetrate her and she licks ~
your bollocks at the same time with a wide open grinning smile!"
I think we're manifesting our extravagant dreams ~ fantasies.
Dab the bag; I believe Baby it's what's in our holographic nut.
'I AM THE MASTER' ~ Levels of Awareness in Consciousness.
"I can see you, I'm aware of you now get in the back and be still!"
Dealing with the Conscious Level ~ 'I can hear the coffee maker'
In the end they're just children sent to beg, they have No choice!
I'm getting off the point, observe the situation fully as a Seer.
It's not there if you don't think about it ~ living in the moment.
It's all going on in the Omnipresence, recognising that 'Thing'
Tuning into changing sensation ~ equanimously feeling feeling.

*

Psyche*delicate * Love

Where can we find the Hippies? I Don't know back in the sixties!
Psychedelic's just a state of Mind ~ Om Psychedelia Substances.
Reprogramming fractality zooming * through my hologram brain.
Couldn't grasp conceptually the vastness of a Psychetropic Ocean.
Understanding Sacred geometry, geomancy, magical mystery.
Fitting it together in the conscious groove ~ Males & females,
spinning chakras, polarised discs, a rutting physical Universe.
It is whatever ~ If you're happy I'm happy; Beautiful diamond.
"That's what started my Volcano nightmares ~ overflowing lava"
Just Programming, know it by breaking out of the Programme!
Morphogenic Field*Cubism's Magnetism, still, white lighting.
A FUN ride in outer space discovering our Inner space.
"He don't give a fuck about having Alzheimer's!"
Cosmic rainbows ~ "You have nothing hidden"

True what they said 'bout It

Not just hanging around Utopia ~ Apsaras in Paradise.
A Cock's a Cock! Don't want the Place of false smiles.
The Bubbly not the Miserable! Gets us out there.....
"And they said they enjoyed it!"

*

Uroplatus phantasticus

All variation on a theme. Who knows what's goin' on in any Lodge?
What to do now? "I f... hope not, just comin' up to my pension, don't
want to be put in a concentration camp and forced against my will!"
Confucius' Virgin brides ~ "they'd never even heard of LSD!"
Who's Not Brainwashed!!!? Ideation ~ Lost in Space.
Putting it in the Navigation....

*

Layla's Night

"People with nothing to lose ~ at your front gate mate!"
They came on the Kabul Super Express, 'Akbar the Great'
A title given to him by the people ~ a beloved name if true
He was a Philanthropist, all for the good of others, it's said.
Being of an Extraordinary potential ~ Somebody has to do it!
Afghani Lines straight thru the gate to the Taj Mahal's front door!

*

The Best of the Best Test

Another Viral Mind Program thinks there's concepts beyond YOU!
Keep reprogramming the system inside your brain, Reboot it again.
"Goa Greed a Big sellout" ~ but still got magic & amazing people!
"Shouldn't we resist evil?" There are No 'shoulds' it's all bollocks!
Is it the best you can do? Simple, Less stress, suffering; I AM.
Making Peace ~ with that Insane Psychiatric Examination.
No reaction, dead silence, integrational ~ Live is Live.

When I was on the bus

Where's that beautiful energy gone ~ what have they done?
Surrendering, entering the rapids ~ lo and behold, 'Whoosh!'
Who wants to be in Marbella on their own? She's Sizzling.
Travelling makes you a listener ~ offloading of all their shit!
"I'm gonna have to get my tin hat and dive in the bunker!"
"I became the Observer not the Doer" ~ stoked with Time!

*

Of my life

"I realised the Significance ~ In it for the long run"
All going on in the head, nothing coming ~ Telepathic Auras.
Having your inner vision turning on ~ finding the high frequency.
Talking to the parrots not only that the parrots talkin' back to her,
telling her what's up! Doing the best you can as a light worker ~
"The dog doesn't bite, it doesn't even bark!" Perfection is boring!
You know how it is! Trapped in Berlin make it as nice as you can.
Maybe we're in Theta sleep going thru worm holes in deep space.
Explaining a lot of our malfunction*Attacked by baby Dinosaurs.
Cloning pigs in Chengdu, praying to Monsanto for GMO in India!
"We're all looking at a glass of water each with an original perspective
but we can all see a glass of water." ~ Serendipity is in its crystals.
Collected ~ connected Consciousness.

*

Not opening another Demon channel

Channels of Goddesses, they Love to save you, leave you happy.
Yoga fallout ~ Why do you come to me if you hate life so much?
Why make me anymore miserable when you can make me feel good?
Why enter my space ~ simple? Letting go of a soul mate with No smile!
If Love was there I wouldn't have to break my attachments ~ Auras.
"I want a boyfriend who'll kill my father, for abusing me as a child!"

35

<u>So Why Not Magnus Frater? <> Freedom is being eroded!</u>
All this money in a few Oligarchs' hands, wondering what to do
with 'It!' Propaganda tools; Enforcing the Rules by those Elites
who made the Rules, the Laws, Conditionings, our Perceptions.
(85 people have more wealth than the poorest 3.5 Billion, ask
Oxfam not the new Global Stasi). Allowing them too much Power!
If you object to goin' to F... WAR that's your right as a human being?
In a Declaration of human rights. The State is trying to take over Life.
Ask Edward Snowden about Thought Police, NSA; Psy Ops, Prisms!
The system stopped working for the people, Natural law gone MAD!
On top of the wheel, at the bottom of the wheel ~ Still going around.
Wanting to know the TRUTH, Knowing what's REAL in existence.
Is it or Is it Not? Eye Contact! Genes asking is there any problem
virus with the Human code. Revolution on the fringes of Genocide!.
What I never liked about a Job, debt servitude, each day same drudge
for our 'Masters of the Universe!' WAGE SLAVERY being Initiated
as a Global Fear, suppression paradigms, on 'The Poorest People'
Throw in some Collateral Murder with Neo Corporate Imperialism!
Don't have to believe me just take a look at Samsara's desperation.
Realise they're your local Mafia. Controlling the people, your kids,
our Planet's future turns into a Dystopian Empire. Do you want this
for your children? We all believe what we, you, me want to believe.
Ask Mohammed Ali "Floating like a butterfly ~ stinging like a bee!"
Locking up a champion Conscientious Objector in an Illegal War!
Crimes against humanity, time to get off your ass & fight for Justice!
Use Anger & pain to break the bondages of depression & repression?
We are the LOVE, it's inside us, connected to this reflection of Truth.
Set your mind free from this Innate Matrix ~ In your heart just be.
For your own security & self-protection try natural enlightenment!

A Liberal - Trained Killer!
It doesn't matter where you are ~ You are somewhere....
Go see a physicist, nutritionist, spiritualist for a diagnosis!
'The most grotesque Terror you'll ever see in a horror film'
Roll up, they make it for people in pain, by people in pain ~
more they have the feeling of pain they're loving it, are you?
There aren't a lot of people relaxing, lying in hammocks!

*

GOA * Vacationing
A Great place to come ~
for some serious dental work!
Vulnerable to the drill going deeper.
"I just have my teeth cleaned and chill."
Ultimately Success is being born taking a FORM ~
Not 'MY' car, just a car without any personal Identificationing.
Folk thinking they have to make it Subjective, Mental projections.
All an Illusion, mad isn't it? ~ We're becoming* Awareness of things!
You react against it so becoming that pattern, process, programming.
Wildebeests' instinctive response crossing a crocodile infested river.
Becoming more Conscious ~ YOU ARE Naturally PERFECTING

*

WTF-Asking for a 'Convenience Fee!'
Multi-national corporations won't put in a nut or bolt until they
own all the local powers ~ first thing they put in their pockets.
The Superior court, Governments, agents acting in the favour of
the Satanists who won the water rights over organic, local farmers!
Don't let your Mind put you in a box, keep it running thru time*space.
Babylon Matrix wallahs ~ developed a GMO formula for Perfect slime!
And his wife's blowing spark plugs out of her head!

Mystery I Us

That's how I live my life ~ Open to the Magic, realising Maya.
I see the Universe that way, an adventure instead of a Trillion
f.... questions ~ How do we manifest it on top of the Plateau?
I don't have to get any swag, the road is straight to the stars.
Why waste 10 minutes never mind 10 years? Being here now.
I'm floatin' around life Capt. Marvelous ~ However we see it.
Spreadin' the light, telling us we're Super human.

*

"I Clocked You"

"Step behind me petit tyrant and do not vex my spirit"
I'm the same I have this mantra ~ Me, Myself, I.
Being able to Observe, there's so much more here.
It's all new, having that joyful Wonder ~ that's on your face.
Love radiantly in your smile ~ downloaded, living in y/our heart.

*

Pet dogs

You go to Goa to meet people from all over the Planet ~
Merkaba our Cosmic, ancient flower of life * Selfie's movie.
You've been turned into a Financial, wage Slave for their benefit!
Security Invasion of your sacred space for your own protection!
All of my cells screaming Against it! Scavengers, you're their prey!
Reboot getting my wide screen completely level, see the big picture.
"We can learn more from a lie than the Truth" ~ Talkin' Life Up yeah,
depends on one's perspective ~ Who's disconnecting from Truth?
They're releasing information to us now that is invisible to us.
Atomic energetic vibrations coming together to FORM Life ~
Transforming the different particles to sustain some stability.
Present ~ here*now. Sometimes you gotta say it, let it out.
"Are you listening to what I'm saying?" ~ They gotta hear it!

Tee*Total * Mescaline

"No, no, no one told me but it was in the Pineal Collader!"
Everyone else knew it was in the Honeybee too..
An Angel as far as I was concerned ~
"He loves his Bible but there's no Church"
He loves Jesus too keeping him on the path!
You Are the I Am ~ It goes beyond in the end.

*

Wars All Over CODEX Alimentarius Planet.

The 'I Am' Discourses, Cosmic Awareness, all about the Love ~
Say like myself our Love is bigger than that because we are that.
And our human experiences opened up y/our Heart Chakra.
Now you've let it go free ~ the Universe only knows Beauty.
Certainly a way to look at Life amidst this Cosmic Chaos.
Not listening to the blah, blah putting people against each other.
"I won't put it out in the Universe ~ It won't pass my lips"

*

It's all good.

She's there to show us what we don't choose!
Standing in the pouring rain… illogical.
"They don't even have their own bed!"
In sheer terror watching the pendulum blade
swinging closer and closer to you!
Thinking about the Pain making it worse.
Tried emotional Torture, what do you want to know?
Any excuse to Terrorize us... Automatic Androids & Drones.
No Empathy... Whoever's got the gun calls the shots!
In the name of God! Who the F… invented that?
"In a world of possessions expression should be free"
"I love a hammock when I'm hammered!"

39

Shakti is Ma

I'm trying to switch her off and get another girlfriend!
Don't forget Shakti she's the Mother of the Universe.
She'll send you a Walk-in Angel,
she'll say, 'You're my best friend'
And she'll heal you; Maybe she'll find Love and stay ~
Without Karma or any Universe ~ Nature is her Shakti.
She's the one who teaches woman about being a woman.
Chanting everyday to Shiva and everything will be Shanti.
RESPECTING, BEING HONEST, 'I AM'

*

She can enter with Parvati

Women not allowed into the Shiva temple ~ 'Om Namah Shivaya'
Shiva Ling on the windowsill, don't get caught up in your own Mind.
"Inspired by women, she don't wanna be herself. I said sorry
and I accepted; I shouldn't have accepted ~ all the flipouts!"
"I am the five senses of Illusion, being able to accept how much of it?"
I can't imagine what's goin' on, gifting back her sight ~ It is as it is.
"I'm on my way to Auschwitz ~ All my love to you!"

*

How we're gonna put it over.

'Four hours work a week enough for a Zulu to have a good life'
We assess, discriminate, judge, condemn, rule in our Temple.
We know exactly what we need to know about that person!
We're not here to Judge, your energies hit me, winding me up!
The answers from the Mind first and the Mind tells us ~
Not listening to the Heart ~ Monkey Mind download.
"Get in your box and shut up!" That's the joy of...
havin' the Space to let it go & live in Synergy ~
That is it ~ "You won't have these troughs"

Angry for Anything!

Everything's possible, no money to eat, they lost her organs!
"You're not stupid if you don't know; You're stupid
if you don't want to know" ~ OK they're just so stupid!
'Death waking up ~ dreams going into other dreams'
"A bottle of Acid in prison, gave them their first drop!"
"& that girl's very loud, this is a hotel not a brothel!"
They get very upset if you f.... with their ego.
"No you never want to be stuck in Chennai!"
Some things are, some things aren't.
When the Psychedelics run out!
'Just be Aware like Anywhere'

*

Universo * Psicodélico

"And we're a bunch of Lotus eaters"
Be strong my friend, shine with light. I'd like to meet Miss Cambodia!
"It's not just about gettin' a fuck it's about gettin' some deep feeling ~"
"I got a girl so I wouldn't be on my own listenin' to all this screaming!"
The stars are all movin', we're all movin' never meant to standstill.
Crossing the sea of Cosmic chaos ~ "My pussy's oozing Love"
Right here right now not thinking about it..... Victory Hill.
You can't twist India to you ~ you have to go with the flow.
Going where it is not where it isn't ~ It's really everywhere!
"Girl babies get thrown out the window ~ Diabolical horror story.
A tribe of bloodthirsty cannibals out there raping Indigenous women.
The older ones walkin' round like they've been shot in the head!
And they get the children to kill each other, so sad; Where is God?"
"We can make more money out of Tourism
than we can being Warlords!"

Following my Spirit-Soul
A good woman offering same gravitational pull of Heart.
Don't lower yourself, be honest having some self respect.
If she loves you she'll miss you & always want to be by you.
Could have been Paradise, it was Paradise; Trusting ~ gone.
Possessed by a demon, got her home & sent her somewhere.
She gave me that inner strength ~ You're a piece of my heart.
The Love of my Life

*

"I saw an angry Shiva"
I saw my friend with Krishna ~ heard the flute in my heart.
Krishna in the centre of a golden light ~
This is God ~ nobody dies, I'm alive! 'Hare Krishna'
Cosmopolitan ~ teaching me to respect all faiths.
My heart drive was already broken ~ so many times!
Shakti went into the Astral ~ left you in the care of Shiva.
It all belongs to the Cosmic Divine.
My Spiritual Opening

*

Instant Karma
"Once they love you, you can walk all over them ~ married!"
"The only way women can reach God is with their husband"
In a way it's insecurity, Complete Control, A total Mind Fuck.
"Wanting to see my partner full laughing not full drama"
Whatever's going on understanding yourself ~
If you're a bad tempered bugger you'll be surrounded
by people who think you're a bad tempered bugger ~
If you're laughing, happy you'll be surrounded
by people who want to give you Love.
Smile by just being thoughtful ~

Disconnecting the Stress

"I looked at it at Face value, taking myself much too seriously!"
Imprinted on my Heart Drive; Have a Shanti shanti experience!
People are nuts, crazy ~ be gentle with yourself; "I Love him"
"I don't want to do it anymore, seeing through all the veils, getting
focus points to let go of that downloading ~ on the Cosmic Journey"

*

You're the Jewel in the Crown

Because of Love I Feel for You.
The Gas exploded in the Castle!
It's not a Program it's an outcaste Voodoo computer.
"When I took an LSD trip I felt Shiva.
I walked in with a Super dream ~"

*

Dr Jekyll & Miss Hyde.

Suddenly she became a Monster, pinhole eyes rolled down.
Possessed full of hate, anger and fury towards me. It's real!
About Mind letting go ~ having to let myself Stop loving you!
Breaking the attachments of respect, passion, trust and devotion.
To someone who Loves you they're giving it back ~ not negativity.
Very dangerous resistance to pains growing ~ let it go, walk away.
Next Please, next adventure; I do that, it's out there. Via con Eros.
These girls don't lie, desire dead in the bed, felt like the Observer.
Watching the Movie ~ You're in it, a metaphor for Consciousness.
The reason you were there as a star; I fucked up with the light ~
If you got the light you're open to accept this, holding it all.
"I haven't woken up in a nightmare ~ she's heading for one;
I've woken in a new World" ~ It's pouring out, I know this!
"That's the way I tick; We were Expansive, we blew the doors off."
They hold you Precious.

Psychedelic Surrealism

You're downloading ~ Egoic reflections getting out of the way, flowing.
The path is just to take you there ~ coming down on the runway.
Whoosh ~ Grounding you, everyone's a multi*dimensional Oracle.
Getting snippets of Inspiration, thought about it, carried on dancing.
The Monkey mind popped up as it does, puts it in your head,
you dealt with it put it back where it's supposed to be ~
The Mind is there to help us work things out. Tom Robbins,
"It was it, you are what you're it, there are no mistakes"
*

Chongin' on a Chillum

Multi dimensional ~ you get out the way and let it happen.
I deserve better than that, you don't have to take me for granted.
Because we've been in Love ~ holding onto the best until it breaks!
Not terrified to end it, letting go, how will I live without your smiles?
Now you've allowed it to be, become whatever it will be ~ Y/our destiny.
Don't need the answer for that * We are the Universe, it will show you.
Put it to bed, its long overstayed its Welcome; Who'd of thought that?
There you go to Magic of the moment. Trusted, taking each other up.
Have to get in that groove, all waves and rhythms, vibrations, music.
I know she's your sister but I can't understand what she's on about.
It's the way you're downloading ~ "I cannot live with what you're
giving me, can't live reducing me into that tiny box, scowling at me.
Everything is shit, out of his comfort factor, drowning in negativity.
You will be what you are at that time ~ don't try and work it out.
"It's not for the Mind ~ it's for the Heart to sort out!"

Where they've been & what they've done?
½ a sugar cube in your tea, we all know what you mean!
Now I'm in the flow ~ we need these Amazing juices.
On the edge ~ of Expansion, Yeah, got a nice UV tan.
Fight or flight, can't we lift things up and have a bit of FUN?
Have to have Inspiration to Live, keeping it going, as you do.
You knew it wasn't good for you then and you know it's not
good for you now ~ Working that lesson out again and again!
Trying to communicate and to Love ~ Yoginis floating around.
Trippers enjoying that, feast or famine ~ We still stayed Sweet.

*

A little Siberian Fairy & Tokyo's Constant Tremors.
Why live as an Eskimo when you can live in Goa?
Om whatever level it will be ~ it will be AMAZING!
REFLECTION ~ Love with it all, gotta stay in it all.
How we're Protected because we're in the HEART ~
"We're here to bring Heaven to Earth" Showing our Light.
He's the Emperor of the pub, who the fuck are you?
Even with that it is PERFECT, You let it go at that.
Keep bangin' yur head against her wall or give it up.
You experienced the Juice of Bliss and you leave it there ~
Not letting it go to the other extremes ~ holding Joy too tight!
The stranglehold of Attachment to the most beautiful experience in
the passionate World ~ Right thought, right vibration, right orgasm!
Why not Celebrate rather than have such intense Competition?
"Greed is good, Property is theft" What's the World comin' to?
Ask the White Dragons, Gnostic Illuminati, the good guys!
And we all live happily ever after...

Living it

That's where the claws are, trying to retract them like a cat.
Road rage, people biting other people's heads off on TV!
People are good don't put the light out because of fear.
Why are we insecure? She wanted a full commitment ~
That's all, emotion ocean, you allowed her to go, be free.
Be in joyfulness, be happy, that's what I wish for you ~
I don't want her to be all screwed up, that's the crazy Mind.
Don't allow it to talk negatively, fear, grief stressing you out,
because you're missing the essential moment ~ Love space.
Painful loss of the last Lover ~ On the way Peaceful Warrior.

*

Prana light Lament

Put myself on the cross man, banged in my own nails. I forgive you!
You're suffering, preoccupied ~ not in the moment, she's moved on!
Brought all those past experiences ~ you're rewiring the brain.
Love your habits; Live & Let Live, purest non-attachment ~
Live every Cosmic experience to be free to break the cycle.
The obsessive addiction; STOP I'm having a beautiful thought!
How much have you to give? Turning the knowledge into Wisdom.
Getting to the joy, she's delighted, dealt with all that, transferred
her LOVE feelings to another ~ let it all go, easy, She's now Free.

*

Caring Is Sharing ~ Not Obsessional Poor Loser

Believing that she'd always love you and you'll never let her go!
Opening the Love channel up ~ all in the appreciation
of this wonderful natural light in the garden of Life.
Feeding our flame all the time ~ giving love back.
You're OPEN ~ Feeling the energy lighting up, it's ON
We have Ignition! The energy that is LOVE in Itself ~

STOP Tormenting Yourself!

Wouldn't mind if he'd kept it to himself but he gave it to me.
Stand up man from this negative, superstitious, dark World!
That can't be misinterpreted ~ Let some life in, it's a release!
When will the Love of my life walk in? The Mind loves all of it.
'It lasts as long as you want it to last' ~ being together vibe.
All about energy levels ~ "Keep it in the Light Love"
Don't close your heart*chakra, connecting the flame
from there through the Love

*

Heavy Breathing

Ploy investing in Robots! ~ 'An empty cell with a light in it'
'There is no hate, no duality to Love ~ Love is Love'
No way I could just walk out, now the Mind I need you.
Had to just sit there and smile as the negativity went in.
No you don't you're already projecting how it will be.
Back off! Just be in Love, don't be fearful, whose selfish ego?
You were resisting, judging, needing, greed, too much Mind.
Forced to put up with shit as I was rewiring my brain circuit.
That feeling's here ~ preoccupied with an old record or not!
Allowing us to grow as people through conscious experiences.
Pressing our buttons, observing what comes out of our mouth.
Not awake slipping into automatic numbness, remote control.
Being part of it, me asking me, get in there on the dance floor.
I have too many conversations in my head, need to let you go.
Where you put your consciousness and Love energy so be it ~
Forget all the shit on its hard drive need to be living in the heart.
Let beauty come in and rediscover yourself, no playing games.
Just be, gushing with your expressions of Love for each other.
Sublimely projecting being into Love.

Global Back Drop

"I've seen Unicorns, in the field next to me rolling a spliff"
If they can turn us on to Coca Cola why not do it for Love?
Flash it up on the hard drive, a download of subliminal bliss!
Absolutely, absolutely people are always giving that Love back.
Interactive not just there with his headphones and Smart I Galaxy.
Reconnecting and give attention to your own heart not a busy mind.
Not talkin' negatively to yourself, a vision of Demons don't project it
onto me. What are we resonating with? Well with Conscious LOVE.
Don't have to take recreational drugs ~ it's not the MDMA.* the trip.
Forget that, it's permanently blissed out in tune with the Universe.
Alert, I put it away when I needed to; These things distracting us ~
Giving the Monkey Mind power of Maya; Freedom to have no puff.
Sitting well with yourself otherwise you can go off on Skid Row!
We're back on an emotional Wobbly Bob.
'To experience Love ~ to Come Alive'

*

Your Emotional Personality

SHOCK! That was then, jumping into FEAR.
"You're Not going to do what you did before!"
"Piss off!" ~ fuelling you with anger and negative emotions.
The beautiful smile stopped ~ why you gonna stay in there?
To get a verbal lashing! They're unaware of it, just in reaction.
Don't be frightened of your Heart, if you stay in the Love you're
fully protected. Heart chakra opening you won't die of heart dis-ease
Monkey-mind, not the heart throwing bananas. We have to thank-you
for pressing those buttons ~ looking at each moment.
You are an Angel ~ Being allowed to live our TRUTH.

In between the Spaces.

If you can't say anything good about the person, Shut up!
What? I purposely don't have a clue, I don't wanna know ~
I won't endorse that fearful bullshit it's not a bubble believe me.
It's conscious reality ~ I believe in the power behind the word.
We're all talkin' about Love ~ Allowing the Full Experience!
"Come on DJ's we need your help to spread this message"
Project this LOVE in your music bringing us up in Grace.
People out there, OPEN, come there to get to that Cosmic Trip

*

Do You know what I mean

Just because you think you can doesn't mean you have to!
There's all possibilities ~ Giving everybody the allowance.
It's over at that time ~ Love can manifest further down
because you're still in it. Not for you to be Thinking about her;
You've been able to step out! Trust yourself.
Find a place where you can spend time together ~
Doesn't have to be anything already on your hard disc.
Very Osho just being in the moment and CELEBRATING
Not having all those pictures on how it should be ~
It's only a delusion of Maya, insidious, so subtle if you're not
in the stillness you won't be aware of it. That's keeping yourself
SHANTI to me.

*

Free Spirit X Empathy Reject.

How can a soul mate ignore & deny y/our LOVE as if you never
ever existed? In reality your feelings you felt ~ fell out of loving me.
I was saying "Show me what yu got!" A cry from my breaking heart!
Not playing any Ego games. What's she representing to the World?

'Personality * Disorders' * (Arrangement from Wikipedia)

These behavioural patterns in personality disorders are typically associated with substantial disturbances in some behavioural tendencies of an individual, usually involving several areas of the personality, & are nearly always associated with considerable personal & social disruption. A person's classified as having Personality disorder if their abnormalities of behaviour impair their social or occupational functioning. Additionally, personality disorders are inflexible & pervasive across many situations, due in large part to the fact that such behaviour may be ego-syntonic i.e. the patterns are consistent with the ego integrity of the individual) & are, therefore, perceived to be appropriate by that individual. This behaviour can result in maladaptive coping skills, which may lead to personal problems that induce extreme anxiety, distress, or depression.

These patterns of behaviour typically are recognized in adolescence and the beginning of adulthood in some unusual instances, childhood. People with BPD feel emotions more easily more deeply & longer than others do Emotions may repeatedly resurge and persist a long time. Consequently, it may take longer than normal for people with BPD to return to a stable emotional baseline following an intense emotional experience. In Marsha Linehan's view, the sensitivity, intensity, and duration with which people with BPD feel emotions have both positive and negative effects. People with BPD are often exceptionally enthusiastic, idealistic, joyful and loving. However they may feel overwhelmed by negative emotions experiencing intense grief instead of sadness, shame and humiliation instead of mild embarrassment, rage instead of annoyance, and panic instead of nervousness. People with BPD. are especially sensitive to feelings of rejection, criticism, isolation, and perceived failure. Before learning other coping mechanisms, their efforts to manage or escape from their intense negative emotions may lead to self-injury or suicidal behaviour. They are often aware of the intensity of their negative emotional reactions & since they cannot regulate them, they shut them down entirely. This can be harmful to people with BPD. since negative emotions alert people to the

50

presence of a problematic situation and move them to address it. While people with BPD feel joy intensely, they are especially prone to dysphoria, or feelings of mental and emotional distress. Zanarini et al recognized four categories of dysphoria that are typical of this condition: extreme emotions, destructiveness or self-destructiveness, feeling fragmented or lacking identity, and feelings of victimization. Within these categories, a BPD diagnosis is strongly associated with a combination of three specific states: feeling betrayed, "feeling like hurting myself" and feeling out of control Since there is great variety in the types of dysphoria experienced by people with BPD the amplitude of the distress is a helpful indicator of borderline personality disorder. Adding to intense emotions people with BPD experience emotional liability or changeability. Although the term suggests rapid changes between depression & elation the mood swings in people with this condition actually occur more frequently between anger and anxiety and between depression and anxiety.

Borderline personality disorder (BPD) is a personality disorder. The essential features include a pattern of impulsivity and instability of behaviours, interpersonal relationships, & self-image. Splitting (thinking in extremes) Chaos in relationships, markedly disturbed sense of identity Intense or uncontrollable emotional outbursts, anger, rage & depression. The pattern is present by early adulthood and occurs across a variety of situations & contexts. Symptoms include intense fears of abandonment, extreme anger, and irritability, the reason for which others have difficulty understanding People with BPD often engage in idealization/devaluation of others altering between high positive regard & great disappointment Self-harm, suicidal behaviour, substance abuse are common. The most distinguishing symptoms of BPD are marked sensitivity to rejection and thoughts and fears of possible abandonment. Overall, the features of BPD. include unusually intense sensitivity in relationships with others, difficulty regulating emotions, and impulsivity. Other symptoms may include feeling unsure of one's personal identity, morals, and values, having paranoid thoughts when feeling stressed, & severe dissociation.

Behaviour: *Impulsive behaviour is common, including* <u>substance</u> *or* <u>alcohol abuse</u>, <u>eating disorders</u>, <u>unprotected sex</u> *or* <u>indiscriminate sex with multiple partners</u>, <u>reckless spending</u>, *and* <u>reckless driving</u>. *Impulsive behaviour may also include leaving jobs or relationships, running away, and self-injury. People with BPD act impulsively because it gives them immediate relief from their emotional pain. However, in the long term, people with BPD suffer increased pain from the shame and guilt that follow such actions. A cycle often begins in which people with BPD feel emotional pain, engage in impulsive behaviour to relieve that pain, feel shame and guilt over their actions, feel emotional pain from the shame and guilt, and then experience stronger urges to engage in impulsive behaviour to relieve the new pain. As time goes on, impulsive behaviour may become an automatic response to emotional pain.*

Interpersonal relationships: *People with BPD can be very sensitive to the way others treat them, by feeling intense joy and gratitude at perceived expressions of kindness, and intense sadness or anger at perceived criticism or hurtfulness. Their feelings about others often shift from admiration or love to anger or dislike after a disappointment, a perceived threat of losing someone, or a perceived loss of esteem in the eyes of someone they value. This phenomenon, sometimes called* **splitting**, *includes a shift from idealizing others to devaluing them. Combined with mood disturbances, idealization and devaluation can undermine relationships with family, friends, and co-workers. Self-image can also change rapidly from healthy to unhealthy While strongly desiring intimacy, people with BPD tend toward insecure, avoidant or ambivalent, or fearfully preoccupied* <u>attachment patterns</u> *in relationships, & they often view the world as dangerous and malevolent. BPD, like other personality disorders, is linked to increased levels of chronic stress and conflict in romantic relationships, less satisfaction on the part of romantic partners.*

Sense of self: *People with BPD tend to have trouble seeing a clear picture of their identity. In particular, they tend to have difficulty knowing what they value, believe, prefer, and enjoy. They are often unsure about* their long-term goals for relationships & jobs. This difficulty with knowing who they are and what they value can cause people with BPD to experience feeling "empty" and "lost". **Psychopathy** is a personality disorder partly characterized by antisocial & aggressive behaviours, as well as emotional and interpersonal deficits including shallow emotions and a lack of remorse and empathy. One diagnostic criterion of narcissistic personality disorder is a lack of empathy, an unwillingness or inability to recognize or identify with the feelings and needs of others. Characteristics of schizoid personality disorder include emotional coldness, detachment and impaired affect corresponding with an inability to be empathetic and sensitive towards others.

*****

Expanding Collectively * Right Timing
Who am I talking about, the dark demons?
My mind making full-on mental-formations.
Keeps on happening, you can't believe it..
Those feelings of Love were Real after all!
Fighting the ID. controller seeing the truth.
At last Conscious of what the Soul really is
Then you see from beyond that ~ Fuck that!
Whatever judgment you made was wrong but
you thought that it was right * Surreal experiences.
Releasing turbulent, repressed memories into the sky.
Her Programming's wiping itself clean of corrupted files
Stalking you into the labyrinth of charred & broken hearts.
No more hiding, realising Light is burning the fleeing Ignorance.
Completely unaware in the Mental state, acting out this Insanity.
Obsessive Ego going back to the natural space ~ Our naturalness.
"Mind blocks out the Whole Universe"

Might be Saved!
She's got no time for you anymore, got another guy ~
Got to transcend all these pain full, wonder full memories.
How can you ask her to help you move on, it doesn't work!
If the boat's sinking, it's useless to stay, take the jump ~
"Don't let them take you for a ride, never too late to learn" You're
getting serious about someone who's not even thinking about you!
It's time you got out of those fairy tales and have no attachments ~
There's no scope for Love there ~ What do you want to suffer for?
"She knows she's causing you pain so how does she Love you?"
Love doesn't wear off what does is Infatuation ~
For Selfish reasons or Selfless service of LOVE.
You reached the last page of your book.

*

Doesn't Really Care ~ No Love Necessary.
Tripping on ½ a bottle of cough syrup, take a little bit more!!
Went for a walk, stop alienating yourself with compulsive stuff.
Vedanta is the end of knowledge ~ beginning of Wisdom.
Don't let Love take you for a ride, being taken for granted.
"She's lying, made her point by giving herself to another man"
A blank page is something you can write on ~ 'Once upon a time
Chemistry is happening ~ Why do you want to stay in the pain?
Give me Peace not more Stress; Healing the heart with a Lover.
Are you still focusing on this closed door not the opening ones?
"Love is a bridge cross it don't build your house on it." Osho.
You Love all ~ Spiritual Love & the physical love will come.
'Stop putting energy into believing that you are manifesting;
Open up to receive that's all ~ It happens when it happens'
Nothing more beautiful than Love. Start worshipping Venus.
Going through the grind ~ coming out shining as a Star.

Keep Watering the Garden

Who do you give Love to ~ the one who gives
you Love or the one who gives you painfulness?
Have to drop the one embracing pain's reaction.
If it's not working for you change your religion ~
"God is equal to Love doesn't matter how many religions,
there is still Love and an Angel is on the way from Venus"
She didn't want to be with you for one reason or another.
If she Loves you what's she doing with another guy?
Love is blind ~ Where's your self-respect as a man?
My endorphins are craving for your moist, wet lips.
Might be Love might not be love, put a human touch.
No revenge; Stick to the Love vibe you still had your FUN.
Don't hang onto hope, hope has gone; Let go of that hope!
How can you Love her now, It's wrong; Don't wanna be
the sacrificial goat for no reason. Be in Love with Love,
change the face, a flower's plucked another grows in its place.
She found out what was more important to her than her Love
for you. When you've got that delicious fruit back in your lap ~
no thought can enter.

*

Addiction's Seduction

There's always people who want more and more and more.
Excellent pain killer, Opium, Morphine, onto the next one ~
Shiva was jealous, used the Cannabis plant to save the Earth.
Locals and High Priests are legally tripping on Bhang ~
We're ruled by the Mind, a slave to our thoughts.
Intellect is the driver driving you insane;
Rising above your emotions, this Maya ~
"Let's have some Poppy Milk lassi"
Colours of Moonlight, silver blue.

"I don't want pain"

He doesn't believe he's in a box, spent so many
years doped up ~ "Which reality is real for me?"
"It'd be a nice place to visit after the Revolution"
Take your money take your dross you can't buy me.
You're not having my peaceful Mind, my SHANTI.
Less altars, less stuff, becoming freer the drugs
don't work anymore ~ going dark, the light's gone out!
Heart chakra mesh, angels grounding, stuck to the garden gate.
To put his energy right he should be out there fully in the light.
Coming from the power of the word, speaking for myself.
No I don't go into their conversations, I'm not here for that.
Seeing myself being sucked out ~ have a word with yourself.
"Got your bottle of water ~ now go"

*

Insatiably eating out yur heart

To give a peaceful life to your neighbours from Hell!
Coke his downfall, feeding his nasty habit, screwed into a box.
Cuts off yur heart not connecting with the feeling inside ~
Your light's being able to ignite your Astral bodies.
That's the one inside ~ Connection to the Cosmic essence.
How can we have a society when it's snowing all over the Planet
because decisions aren't from the heart, way of a Peaceful warrior?
Empathy, treading lightly, respect, being in the Grace ~ Smiley face.
"I Love you, please forgive me, I'm sorry; I Love you"
"Am I inwardly feeling comfortable in my own skin?"
This wasn't me, getting the joy back, whole again.
He's too fearful, he holds it so tight, strangles it to death.
Everyone released through telepathy ~ 'As we intuit it, it is, as
we say it so be it.' So watch your words.. "I'm losing my mind!"
Cancel it and get that off your hard drive!

Dropping Through

If you can go through an acid trip with something eating
your brain and blasting your emotions then you'll be ok!
"I'm confused if I love you or if I don't love you" What's it mean?
Grab it by the balls and be passionate, coming together as before.
Love is not a concept, it's opening to sharing deep, intimate feelings.
"I went to Ibiza for my honeymoon ~ I still got the pictures"
Everybody wants something, expectations of a conditioned mind.
Why not live like you're on holiday all of the time? K. Gibran,
'Love Life to be intimate with Life's innermost secret.'
'Love is the offspring of spiritual affinity'

*

Starts to be less and less

"I do not project this onto myself ~
"I'm not asleep, I'm conscious and I'm giving it to myself"
It's the thought going off, now we're on the trip.
"How can it be the Love if you're in the fearful box?"
You can see this ~ Wants to open the box
and see the addiction inside.

*

What's Up?

"I Love Lookin' behind the eyes of Babylon"
Aren't you living if you haven't got a bag of worries?
Skinning up, I can hear him, his thoughts talking to my head.
Here have it back, always telling other people what to do!
Wanting to offload everything he gave her ~
Putting the hooks, rites and rituals in the sea.
Sadhus sitting in glacial caves ~ super Powerfully.
On the other plane ~ meditating, turning the furnace on!
Left the Temple ~ transcending to the Astral dimension.
"I Love with kindness all the time"

Pricked it

Releasing stuff you're bringing up in you ~ Look at Yourself!
Why did I? Now what's that all about? I don't get lost in it ~
I've clocked it, I know right in your Conscious, your full frontal.
Just the fact that you've witnessed it, that's the Cracker!
You've popped the bubble, you're out of that matrix sphere ~
Experienced it, released it & you didn't see the bubble anyway!
Not allowing this bending mind to play with the Loading of this
word 'LOVE' should be their Mantra not an addicted obsession!
Blossoming seeds of deluded aspiration and we think this stuff
is the expression of life ~ It just closes down our Inspiration.
Throw it up to the Universe ~ Trust in Love's revolution

*

Heart ~ Locket

If Shakti is strong she can see this guy's heartbroken in his eyes.
When I hear heart break stories ~ Those human emotional waves.
"I had to Love her to let her be free" She's already broken the bond.
Be in This moment ~ I'm on this Plateau ~ I've lived my life to here.
I've built that box, a minute cardboard box around myself.
I can't shrink my life into that with you because I know ~
And I can't come into that box! Energy of no fixed abode.
On your load not on my downloading ~ of miscommunication.
It can be all around me but I'm being Unconditional Love.
Reminding myself to Stop the drama and be in the light.
The darkest Angels coming to show us another World.
Made me aware it wasn't my World; Thank Heaven.
And appreciate how Loved and blessed I am ~
When I hear heart break stories.

Global Net of Control

Barcoding laser 3D printed tags onto babies. DNA databased
The illusion you're winning the game but you're unaware of it!
Cameras taking over, not for the good of people but the Boss.
Why do they need to know that when you're not a criminal?
Obsessed Love pulled the rug from under my arse ~
STOP watching that shit and tune into Planet Earth!
What's happening when we don't live in the Love?

*

They Take - They Suck!

"I'm the only one who is OK, what do you do?"
She's getting on with it, full steam ahead! 'Be here now ~
Still feeling those deepest attachments ~ what d'yu expect?
Put a new face to it, it will change as her deliriously hot arse.
It won't be rainy season forever the Sun will come again ~
A Goa sunset, she's really left me for another vision of desire.
Experienced it before ~ Standing in your truth consciousness.
You can't be emotional about your Lover who goes to bed with
someone else. Standing by the Ocean hoping she'd come back!

*

Wake Up Call

'Message to a Light*worker ~ A continuous flow'
I fell into that dream that we were in a Love paradigm.
You yearning for my kiss ~ that we'd always be in this bliss.
Poetic muse left on the shuttle, it's changed like the Universe.
Life is suffering, I don't go for that but It is if you want it to be.
Don't make any plans.... This isn't Love this is Adoration!
Been in Love with Love herself ~ It comes in many forms.

On our way to the Outback.

He played Mind games, we were Expansive, exploring, having Fun.
It didn't intimidate me, I could handle it ~ back at the Pivotal Point
where I could shoot through and unravel the jumper; It's just
letting it go, letting it go, letting it go, letting it go, letting it go ~
& your Mind Loves it - "You're not good enough, blame, Inferiors!"
No joy in a Cynic's mind and they wipe people out in brushstrokes,
all that bollocks, telling me about his arthritis; I told him to fuck off!
"Haven't you got any arthritis, why haven't you got arthritis dear?"
Don't project onto me, I don't know you, they're not for me to meet.
He took himself to the darkest place like a Badger.
"There's a Pill for Chemical imbalance, keepin' them tickety boo!"
Filled with all this light dispels the dark.

*

Light Shield

Truth's my Protection; from Riots to Love & fluffy ecstasy brownies!
"Come at me and I'll come at you!" ~ In my Boadicea war chariot!
This night I'm flying fully in the Spirit, didn't want to come down.
As soon as I heard, "let's take her home" I took off like a Gazelle.
Right age for a punk I think he's Hofmann whizzing past the Temple.
Easy on your own keeps yourself centred. "You're as cool as Fuck!"
"If it's snowing in India it's gotta be snowing all over the Planet"
And he takes uppers, downers, he takes Sniff, he's in a dream ~
Kept herself clean or a one way street into the opaque darkness.
All these lovely people stuck to this shit! A chronic alcoholic fit;
Showed me why you never hit women and children ~ Daddy!
'When he was on the drugs he was alright then he went on
the drink and coke and turned into a messy, wild animal'
'Now Coca everybody's mean, seen the demon!'
Coke and drink Heart attack Central.
Losing the Goa Psychedelic vibes ~

Lovely Not Ugly * Object Metaphor
Coming from an Open heart, Cosmic lore, aligned with Life.
"We're trying to portray the light ~ We Are the Light!"
All the rest is Maya, bollocks, delusion, enslaved in it, a cage!
Paid Friday, skint Monday. Full of beans, full of the wrong beans!
Jumping into Fear with a Monster, Satan the darkest, scariest.
Being Conditioned, pressing all our buttons on my Download.
Patterns in the sand, at that moment ~ time for Introspection.
Just throwing in the Love ~ get it in there, get it in there

*

Musical Feathers
I was fully in flight perching on different wave crests ~
You gotta let it go, can't think for her, being Honest to you!
Looking after yourself feed your Soul ~ not a shrunken skull.
Now I stand back and wait because the Universe will show me
especially if there's no one sitting on your head having a drama!
It didn't take her to her knees ~ knows it's on a higher Plane.

*

Nikola Tesla ~ Super high connection in the sky
'If you want to find the secrets of the Universe ~
think in terms of energy, frequency and vibration'

*

Tough As!
Shiva Valley Energy Core not full of Uncle stag parties!
Insatiable, "He was there, couldn't play, too twated!"
Let's all bring it out, the Love; Red hearts full of compassion.
Love Now ~ next move, let's see what the Universe brings in.
Big Bellied Gay Biker Buddhas in the twilight zone ~
Do I really owe you an apology? No, good fun with yu mates.
A gift to the Gods, left my £100 Airwaves outside the Temple!

<u>The World of Sniff</u>

Give em what they want, get them out your life as soon as possible.
They'll only tell you about themselves; Like Shagging chicks on Ice!
Don't try reasoning with them ~ they're too high to come down.
"Mescaline is more spiritual than Acid, in touch with everything"
LSD is more cartoon, can invent an apple computer, envisage DNA.
There are people with consciousness and there are people who
have no consciousness, no feeling, no understanding whatsoever.
Living with a different projection, perception, reflection, reaction.
Alcoholics in Shiva's Valley, not creative dancing but exorcising.
Not looking into each other's eyes ~ sharing rainbow tribal vibes.
"Does guilt run in the blood?" Stop looking in the mirror!
Year of the horse get on the Ket! Speed Psychosis try Solaris.
'Don't hate, meditate, eat Acid see God' Champagne Charlie life-
style, "Come on, come on ~ you know you want to be tempted!"
Doing it on the hoof, blasting it ~ of course you'll come down,
another little toot, toot, toot ~ before you know it you're in
bed with the Badger! "This is Anjuna home of the party
for sure they're gonna knock on your door one day."
When you're out there peaking it's hard to keep it together.
"I haven't come here for all this shit with the law & the wife!"
It has an effect especially on Hippies ~

*

<u>Oh, here we are back in this f...... movie!</u>

Helicopter Money ~ just Giving the money away it's so worthless!
Alcohol, what a waste of a life; why? And I got deeply hurt...
Thank God I've walked out of that Cinema....
How about seeing the bigger picture? 'Kushdibok'
Not getting this Love Fix ~ whatever you call it!

THE END!

It's been a complete movie & I've just walked out the Cinema.
Love's not got to hold onto people, that's right even our kids!
I can't hold you ~ that's this 'be here now vibe'
KEEP IN the LIGHT *not stuck in the Twilit zone.
Not to judge them ~ there's a Pill out there.
The right chemical * reaction in your brain...
Indulged all your tantrums; Wait and watch.
Her little heart going ~ 'bump bump bump'
*
**

Sweeter than a Sugar Cube

In the multi dimensional * don't project anything allow it
to be what it will be if it's not the picture we've set down,
we're gutted, You know what I mean? We're not in the now.
I'm not here I'm over there ~ Don't project that onto me.
Positive reinforcements not Alcohol fuelled Aggression!
Girls ordered to marry the Rapists who had violated them!
They hate you all of a sudden! "But I'm not doing anything!"
Escaping the delusion that you were ever in Love & Loved.
Light goes & a bit of paranoia's bypassing the heart chakra.
Not spiritual, can't Love anymore, not talking, she can't stop!
Don't tell me I've been dumped again! We are all in Love!
A flash of Inspiration... "That's My train!"

*

*8.5hz Binaural Psyche Baba * Cosmic Inshallah Super Shanti.*

Solfeggio frequencies ~ 174Hz, 285Hz, 396Hz, 417Hz,
528Hz, 639Hz, 741Hz, 852Hz, 963Hz ~ Positive shifts.
Deoxyribonucleic Acid, DNA. ~ 'To see the one in all we see'
Different intensity ~ Vibrational tones of Cosmic Universes.

She's a Love

Magic ~ You see these little things and they're twinkling at you.
Who needs any Agreement? I hadn't even unpacked my bags!
Dramas and dross and negativity all around ~ on the jitter.
You tried to put me in a cardboard box! Not True to himself.
He's still in that camp but she's moved on ~
They're Demons until they're standing in the light.
Just need to connect with the LOVE not any dark World.
A breath of relief, back in my little shack beside the Ocean.
What a wonderful way to be woken up!

*

Living It

We do not protect our innocent children ~
Don't lock them up; change the hard drive!
Sending Love instead of sucking up loss, anger and hate.
Stuck to it can't get out of it ~ surely we'll find some release.
"They're Christians they're allowed to think more than others!"
700 years of bloody inquisition, Obeying the rules of discipline!
Demons are leaving. Hooked, flood it with light, let's just ZAP it!
Turns Obsessive when you've lost control over your Idol!
The figure of your Attachment. Kissing the Holy white Meteorite.
Confused, can't work it out, ending up thinking I must love him!
Whilst you're getting your fix you're in it, if not you're out of it.
It's all vibration in your head space ~ these things like Boomerangs
we throw them out and Bang it comes in. Be careful what you desire.
Lowering your self-esteem, repeating your Hard drive, Manifesting!
Just become the Observer.. like giving it a good wash because that
jumper doesn't fit you anymore. Until you get it out the closet,
look at it you don't know it's there ~You've outgrown it,
bigger than that! Do you know what's being created in your
Subconscious here, now? So you get a new one ~ one that fits.

Magical Roundabout Packed with Totty.

"We are all under Psychological Attack!" Up pops Black Ops...
Rolling fog comes thru the house; Is it too late to be a Mason?
That wasn't a horror story was it? Thank God I missed that one!
Head over the tank, no helmet, screwing it to death 0-100 in 7 secs.
A Pocket Rocket her 4000 tongue parts working in Perfect harmony
Try nitrous oxide balloons, Happy Herb or a Psychedelic pizza,
Codeine Pujas; Skinning up they even brought me an ashtray!
There are people in the world who do not give a Fuck!
"What if we do die will that bother an ant?"
Ants outnumber humans 17 billion to one. Stopped at Customs
last thing you want is a dog sitting next to you pointing at you!
40 years for a bag of Poppers! They come to Goa to try Acid.
Out of Control, Nuclear reaction taking out the Solar System!
Codes of Cosmic Nature ~ "We've earned the right to be here"

*

One Too Many

Drugs of our time ~ waves of emotions flooding through.
They're feeling better if you're drinking with them!
"Here have a drink, what's the f.... matter with you?"
"It won't harm, it won't hurt you, legal!" Hey chill your beans!
My experience of pissheads, every English pub is full of 'em.
We're all damaged, bring it on, I can look at it, deal with it...
Consciously as I am now ~ It's stepping back, it's letting it be.
If You can't refuse the addiction then you take 2nd place to it!
In the next breath ~ You don't exist then you get over it again,
then SLAMBANG! Covering it up, that's Fuckin' Abuse!
Seeing a smile ~ I don't want to analyse too much.
which new generation's on marching powder?
I want to walk with someone fully in the light!
All the lovely Psychedelic people have left ~

ATTACHED SO DEEP

"I am quite happy even when shit's flyin'" ~ Angered and suffering.
I used it as fuel to help myself, to propel me out of the dramas!
Difficult to resist light. Why you comin' down to upset yourself?
And I've told you to Fuck off!! It got messy.. toughest emotions.
It takes time to get these hooks out of my deepest tantric auras.
I know she was in it she broke and told me how sorry she was.
Going through her rigmarole, rewiring patterns of hard-drive...
Well that's being in the moment ~ Omniscience, omnipresence.
And we talk about here or over there ~ not in the Cosmic flow.
The Monkey Mind pulls us in a scenario, theatre, play, show going
off in the head, obsessive regurgitating stuff and it's Not Real.
Being here now ~ in this moment, not making any more dramas!
YOU ARE IN THIS MOMENT NOW ~ FEELING YOUR HEART
STOPS THE MIND THINKING ~ BEING ESSENTIAL SPACE.
Letting it go into Stillness ~ filled with Universal Love energy.
Not even a shame, 'It was what it was' I miss You addiction.
The Creative Cosmic Connection, what else is there?
Most tender Intimacy.. Things changing in the grace.
Hooked straight away ~ "don't worry about me lovely"
YOU GOTTA STAY ~ BE IN LOVE WITH IT ALL!
You're saying to One person, giving them yourself, Soulmate.
Don't be saying this gotta be forever ~ staying in the Truth.
Not your emotions, it's everything else, expanding the Universe.
Not talking the dross, not why it didn't work on the hard-drive...
Be in Love with the instant of the experience, what we're here
to do ~ To be in Love, to be the Love and Shine the Love.
And let the light shine through you. If you're not in the Love how
can the Love shine through you? It's cheated you out of the Bliss.
I'm Alive and Thank You; I've been the Observer all the time ~
BE * EXPERIENCING * JOY ....being in that smile

Welcome to Goa

'Went in as PsyTrance Babas came out as Electro Tourists!'
I think it liked the screaming! A frog jumped up her arse.
"LSD it's something you do as a teenager in a field"
You make 'em you break 'em! No class what's goin' on?
'Anti-virus, don't let NSA. see what you're doing. Limited offer,
33% off' Making me invisible. Everybody has it, who told you?
It was Painful, it is but you have to get on with it!

*

It's TOXIC for Everyone!

Intimacy not Conspiracy; Crystal Maze onto Level 10,
sitting on your head, Zaps all your energy!
I got my life back, holistic Gaia in natural synergy.
"It comes in through me ~ goes out through her."
"I am the beginning she is the end"
Soulmate soulmate soulmate soulmate free.
Still gotta be able to let it go ~ emotional waves.
Otherwise still rattlin' the cage of the Mind.
Just a word for your nuttiness.

*

What's pressed your buttons?

We see it with our eyes and our Mind gets hold of it in trauma.
"She never even left me a note!" "Never said she had a lover!"
You've moved on ~ it's happened to us all, we can all relate.
We can let it go because we can. You have Trust in yourself.
Gifting Closure, You're letting go ~ having to let go, no choice.
Times to realise where my Love sits being a conscious human.
The Love is Inside us ~ You are the Love, we're all in Love.
It doesn't disappear when she walks out on you full of fear.
We're here to experience ~ I left it like that!
She is a reflection of her light in yours

I was laughing with a Nomad of the Universe

At this age I think these things are funny. Devastated ~
I'm not taking you that seriously! I had to break my heart!
So much commitment; No it is what it is, on the hard-drive.
Let's hope it works, it does, have to allow yourself it.
When I've worked out I got a 'Wobbly Bob' on because
It's all perfection ~ it's all perfection.
Each time we have Angst it's because of our heart-drive. So I
don't have Angst anymore; I won't like you for taking me there!
Having a bit of wisdom by stepping away, now deal with
the feelings of stepping away! Bring them on, thinking of
'What the bleep' ~ then I can rewire the brain, fully conscious,
of what we've taken in, what we haven't realised of the fact
that that is happening. We're Not told to be Aware, coming
from a World of doing, doing, doing ~ If you're not reacting
you're doing Nothing! This relationship has become Toxic.
Don't know about quiet, still, calm Meditation ~
Trying to communicate what they'll understand.
How we are aware of it is the key. He likes his bubble!
"Not seen you for a long time because you've been in nick"
Unlucky in Love! ~ What did you do to make that Love?
"In India if you don't own a necklace shows you're not Loved!"
"Well I Am Loved!" The Love is alive inside all of us ~ be together.
It's a sign of being Loved, Loved by Shiva, we're Loved by all of it.
Give it a name or not, Space, a tree, seas, our Sun, my Goddess
Loved by all of it, we're here, everything is here because of Love.
When that special person leaves your life falls apart. Still grieving.
Talkin' the talk to yourself making ourselves weak with distraction.
Zips it automatically across the super fast ice, we've done it before.
It's inside you, it's not in Anjuna, Goa, it's where you are, here now.
Going with the no-mind flow ~ being in that moment all together.

Non Premeditated

How can we look at anyone else and say ~ 'Blah?'
We're here for ourselves, being here with ourselves;
Stop the monkey mind ~ it's going quiet, why have I got
to be pulled into the TV. All the dramas keeping me busy
all that time ~ wasted on a looping hologram. Rewind,
Play, Fast Forward, Delete, Reset to the Now again.
Tormenting yourself to death, you gotta let it be ~ it'll be
what it will be, that's what I had to do, not right or wrong.
Not here to judge it ~ let it be, know you are the Love inside.
How the light shines through, diving in, came to critical mass.
In situations there's no answers just be beauty, exquisite Love.

*

Clarity not dark, skanky moments.

I can't apologise for being in Love, they've lost that connection.
Always talking Life here for good stuff, higher stuff full of joy.
Staying in the Bliss, everyone's got their own Level of Truth.
Keeping in Cosmic Love, we're Loved and Loved and blessed
Loved and Loved every nano-second ~ this is truly who we are.
"I believe in Love" ~ deep in the groove of One person.
Not expressing it to just one person; Releasing it all!
Allowing you to be ~ whatever * Love it all Satsang.

*

Energy Meditation Darshan

"The most spiritual thing is to laugh" Ha Ha Ha!
Full on all the time ~ telepathic with ET. dolphins.
Alien eels if you catch them they'll bite your hand off!
I agree we are the Gods, Siesta all the same quality to be ~
They got married in a prison, all their friends were locked up!
He just loves getting mangled, all smacked up, wobblin' about!
"We're only three meals away from anarchy!"

Intuitive Intimacy

"It's so beautiful" ~ Opening your heart & vulva chakra.
Told me so many times that she wanted to leave me!
Not feeling it anymore ~ Are you aware of your Mind?
Listening to your Mind rather than feeling your heart.
You have to lose everything you love, the most precious, to know.
"When you're left with that hole in your heart"
Cancel that don't project it onto me!
Transmuting mind over heart ~
*

Aphrodite's Broken Heart

You live in beauty, you walk in that beauty ~ Heart chakra....
Bypassing a Devious Zone, holding up the Truth ~ Your Truth.
Sending it all positive energy response ~ "I'll hold up my corner"
*Ultimately being in the now * the heart without any axe to grind.*
He really loves you, you must go back to him ~ Making it all up!
A dark Master sucking her dry not opening any gates to Heaven!
Having to step away into the Space apart ~ Love's Cold Pussy!
*

STOP THE THOUGHTS & YOU STOP THE EMOTIONS

By stopping the story going on in their head; ~ "Oh I'm Fucked!"
DMT. 'Dance Music Therapy'- It's not the person it's the process?
Stop everything happening for your egoic, shifting Consciousness
into the light. 'You totally accept loss then you experience 'Anatta'
This is the one who makes you feel that extra special blissfulness.
All in the heart, programmed to feel your way through it!
"Women move on easier ~ different for us to lose our addiction."
Banged the hooks in hard, the last nail, the one you needed!
*Being in the now leaving Venus * "You can walk away in Peace"*
Boxed it off ~ Gone, free.

It's All a Vortex!

A change of reality ~ who are you, next to me, inside me?
Testing what we're feeling, what are we all attracting ~
It's so beautiful ~ Opening your heart chakra with me.
Having the gratitude for all the mercies and delights.
"Somehow I've attracted all these Pleiadian vibes"
Reality check, she needed to move on, happy!
Affirmations ~ looking in the Intimacy Sutras.

*

Vicious the sausage dog

We've been through the ringer, fully mangled!
Lost a Jewel, "I never walked out on a woman"
Neurotransmitting to fulfill dreams in her heart.
Her Mind full of expectations & deep insecurities.
Blocked me, Now you're free ~ I don't wanna be free,
why would I wanna be free? To Love again telepathy!
She's broken the link, made love with someone else!
I led her to her destiny ~ she's gone from my heart forever.
Poetic tragedy, gotta let her go, if you want to see it like that.
When you can't stand it anymore & she don't care, realise why!
I don't see holding onto only beautiful memories ~ be here now

*

Divine Laddu

Love is not about making choices; Give it conscious respect.
If she's gone she's gone ~ She's transmuted her heart.
Doesn't mean LOVE has gone, it doesn't belong to her.
She can't take it! Love can't be so f....... painful can it?
Can't be, must be something else sweetheart! "At the end
of the day I had the best times of my life with you Baby"
Lovers' energy ~ If she don't want it you can't give it.

Not what's on our Download?

It lies within each of us so we can't blame anyone else! Like You!
All you need is one dodgy prawn! Time we have to enjoy 'Self'
In the Allowance ~ In the Love ~ You can Love to Love.
"You've been found!" ~ "I was never lost Babe!"
"Manic he's only used to being adored!"
If that's Love in that House of Horrors...
Lives in that world, all his girlfriends were burnouts!
A bully, because they're lost in the World of Sniff!
It eats the heart of people, detaching the human feelings.
Takes you over the edge of darkness, they're mean, insatiable,
full selfish, full ego, full sex, full fucking! Does he like Coca?
It's not like MDMA ~ Opening the heart chakra's Lotus petals.
That's supposed to take our Mind into the Heart ~ Merging
You must Relax!

*

Words are Vibrational

Whistlin' inside ~ If you truly Love them you'll let them feel free to be
Soul connection. "Have to TRUST their wishes because I love her"
Told the Universe, 'I don't know what to do ~ in your hands now'
It's to do with love but it's not the one you want to be with.
Cutting through the true feelings ~ no negativity in a nutshell!
"You have to be happy, anyway I didn't make them unhappy!"
*" ~ I WAS IN HAPPINESS ~" * " ~ I AM HAPPINESS ~ "*
I was still tripping couldn't let go, when do you say it's over?
"They'll play until Keith Richards drops dead on the stage!"
Respect and honesty, if you Love yourself; Watch This Space!
Total Peace of Mind, no resistance then you got 'No Mind ~
Love is Love ~ In essential Love there is No hate,
no duality to Love ~ no You and me ~ Ultimately

Communicate On the Planet

'Measurement of humanity was how slow they'd let you die'
There are reasons she leaped into a deeper pudding! What
a harsh sketch, left a lot to be desired! Need a Love Harem.
Stressed, cold shouldered, somehow I was in the doghouse.
Needy, doing it for ulterior motives I knew It def. wasn't right.
She went, I was shocked when she said she was engaged!
She was taking the piss! You're a good girl, might be ~
utterly useless at some things, he took her under his wing.
She's over the infatuated Moon ~ My Love is no less...

*

"It Feels Like a ZOO!"

Don't blow my Mind blow my hot pulsations ~ "I Love your Cock!"
"Chicks' weaknesses for Cocaine; Selfish, EGOIC, Only for Yourselves"
"Don't underestimate the POWER of Coke ~ Heart ~ Mind-Alterations;
One Line & That pain is gone into Oblivion * Untruth's Tragic Love!"
"She'll be there until the last lines are gone ~ follows you like a puppy"
Better for Sex, she wants the Full Attention Centered on her; It isn't the
Real Thing! Reprogrammed all their emotions, auras, Loving promises!

*

Fully Hidden Ego Tripping

Completely, unspoken story ~ 'The Secret Life of Coke Adulterated'.
"I Am ~ The Collateral Damage of M/y/our Love's * Vivid delusions!"
Love Predator, criminal ~ eyes flaming in a field of Vital Negativities.
As guilty as Unconscious Sin, no truth can't look me in the face, eyes
full of Lies inside a Crime Passionelle * justifying all y/our Ignorance!
You're burning the wings of your devoted Angel ~ 'In La Kech'
"It is what it is" * "And what is that then?" "This ~

Come to Goa and Get Wasted!

Falling into a naughty Temptation with a very teasing smile ~
Wicked cut out my beating heart, left it on a road to Delusional!
Getting what you wanted ~ living a Massive lie in your Soul, no?
It is what it is, is it? Chop me another line of Un/consciousness!
*Betrayed and not blaming an untrue reflection * She's Perfection!*
Feeling Sunrises of my Intuition ~ knowing what isn't Really Real.
*You let all the Magic go * for more of the bliss of your Innocence!*

*

Next to a Predator.

"You mean Israelis on our patch?" "We're not having that!"
"They're organised man and there's always a Nigerian"
There's always Mr. Innocent, rolls up, surly and hard,
supporting his own habit; Over the limit of temptation,
getting anything you want, here to play, already got a big appetite!
No way there can be anymore, they weren't pharmaceutical either.
Looking out for each other that's what makes it safe in Anjuna.
Nothing to do with innocent and naive, this is going too far!
Blood sugar all over the place, moods swinging erratically.
If you don't know you don't know .... that it's a Full Stop!
It all started with me travelling wearing a strawberry red turban.
Someone who showed affection for my sisters ~ fully in tears.
A wildly spinning Top, scared of himself, a danger to himself.
Wrap yur head and keep yur cool; You can have Head fry!
Nobody knows where I'm from, you can Peak in this heat.
It's happened for a reason we'll ascend here in the light.
If I am the light warrior I trust that I am
there is only the Light heart.

<u>Step back Sweetheart</u>
Releasing ourselves from our Temple
walking out through the doors ~
Opening up to the * LOVE Milky Way *
On your knees calling on your inner strength.
Helping each other transcend ~ Transcend what?
Your mind full of amazing, greedy delusions.
Gave her a healing, fought off any demons.
Living in our Universe, multi-dimensional Affirmations.
Dysfunctional Lord of the rings; 'I'm ok you're not ok right?'
Burning in the light coming back in with the purity.
Having respect standing in my truth and your mind open.
What happens that is truly who we are not the dross.

*

<u>Everybody's ^ feeling ^ the same</u>
Woke up on top of the Hummingbird Pyramid.
Nothing happens without your permission ~
Twangled, on the mat having a masala chai.
You must taste for what you really want
That picture's being downloaded, saved.
How much we reflect that inner voice.
Super aware of Self ~ Love essence.

*

<u>Surfing Bhakti</u>
Fractographic physics as pure Psy-poetry.
Let it absorb all light * inserting the Crystal.
Sending in your truth ~ Unified hologram.
Light will work in us to dispel the darkness.
Another Romantic tragedy how can that be?
Light coming through ~ You Are Loved Baby.

"You can fight the darkness or you can light a candle"
"I don't know how I feel about anything anymore"
Lost in the same vast sea looking for each other ~
You go into Consciously or does Consciously come to you?
The more nothing you can do, the stronger Theta it gets.
Aligning me in the moment ~ It just happens, true love.
Love is not lazy ~ Active Feelings, sharing it.
You believe it, channel that makes you happy.
Light rays falling on a leaf from a parallel dimension.
Give up your bondage by being in this present ~

*

Popcorn Mufti.
"I talk so much shit, prancing round the holy yard ~
Whatever life gives you, it's for you." "It's nice in here."
Go into the shadows to see the auras' ~ raising vibrations.
WTF can't cope with adoration. FGM. culling a sweetheart's clit!
Why is there so much negative Propaganda about fidel Muslims?
#8 Majjid street, Inshallah, with a bit of luck, God willing, Salaam.

*

No should, would, could about it!
Sense of Individual, Sense of One.
Just feeling it all ~ Full on SENSATION!
Consciously Illuminating all the Forms.
Because there's nothing to achieve.
They're looking Out missing the Inside ~
Om Shanti Shanti, It's light ~ it's got wings.
It All is One experience ~ fully the same same.
It's all me, my suffering ~ just an aspect of Love.
All I'm doing is reminding myself ~ remembering what it is.
Wanting something to Achieve we achieve nothing in the end!
When they kneel down in the waves ~ that's a lovely moment.

Star Role

You of little faith ~ everyone's playing their own part.
Illusion being exposed, closer to the Grand Finale!
Are we staying in this drama, anticipating the next episode.
We got it all here and now ~ Clairvoyant beings vibrating.
In that space of super sensitive truth, kissing your mouth.
Feeling our telepathy ~ what do you desire most darling?
Egocentric-Mind transmuting over the heartfelt attraction.

*

I'm Very Light Sensitive

And this Angel's as sweet as a Psychedelicate Shamanette.
I've put this flame out ~ The Universe showing me the way.
He's full of Coca and full of drink and he goes off!
He makes pictures in my head, became a nightmare.
They've given me spliff after spliff and I was wiped!
There's no way I'm going with a time bomb like you!
There's an acrid smell ~ when they're chasing dragons.
Like Marilyn Monroe's, uppers and downers all the time.
Full Power ~ going past that, can't shut yourself down,
too wired, high, need to sleep, need to process all the bits.
Take some Valeries!

*

Your Life is your dream

The Acharya of sperm living in Venus * Fully Sensational!
Made a mantra to the Sun god, impregnated by an Alien!
'Detached Lovers the best and you're also FREE' ~
You wanted it! Not hanging onto someone, not stuck in it.
Unless you like Hell after Heaven, I'll overcome that feeling.
'Obviously you don't need a nice, simple husband if you're a
Star Goddess * meet a Shakti Earth mother * I'll be transcendent

Negative Plane

She Killed it, a dagger straight in the heart; Revenge attack!
This has been hatching for awhile in her subconscious needs.
The Universe brought all the elements together for it to exist.
When you say "fuck it all!" I'm transmuting to get what I want.
'Magnanimously You led her to her destiny' You, now forgotten.
I had to disconnect from the addiction of my serotonin's desires.
Want to feel you on top of me in realms of unquenchable orgasm.
Are you still thinking about it in your head ~ waves of wet emotion.
"Don't Focus on one closed door you won't see many open doors"
Don't Focus on her gorgeous memory either!

*

'New ~ Changes of Reality'

"She's not with the one she Loves; She doesn't Love herself then"
She's certainly not thinking of me only the sense of Impossibility.
It doesn't matter, WHY? You are going to miss her lovely smile ~
Need to distract my Mind, take it off all the attachments to her.
Maya, what has destroyed the dreams of my Goddess of Love?
It's delusional ~ all this is to take you away from your Higher self.
Does she want you to be in Peace? How honest is the sky, Why?
You want to stay depressed or you want to stay in the sunshine?
"I've been getting sexual chemistry from some ecstatic cheeks"
Sets you Free, You don't want to hang onto that Fantasy, right?
Monkey Mind's swinging from branch to branch for mango fruit.
Mind is jumping from thought to thought, confusion and clarity ~
Jumping to the future, past, not being in the now*Love frequency.
Instead of deep Loss and pain she could help me to transcend it.
Returning me to 'Cosmic Love' ~ left in Denial this Love energy.
"From the Heart you don't leave the person for dead"

Off-Loading*True Sufism
Saw her sliding down the pan during my Kabuki ~
Just need to get a grip.. tell your Mind to Wake up!
A Happy plant, change is lush for a lovely light being.
She's been too busy, I want her to be Conscious now.
Need to be kind to yourself ~ Why not just keep it nice?
Never wanting to lose you. We are in this Heart together.
How do we get to any common ground
at the No Hope Heartbreak Motel?

*

As you do it will be
Duality Crap ~ love, anger, moving into a different new era.
'It is as it is' ~ Singular & multi-dimensionally fitting together.
Let those thoughts go and come into your Heart; Let's dissolve.
Another download coming in again, gotta let it go, gotta let go ~
*Be in Space*Heart *Have to face it* We are the Masters of Self*

*

Specks of Stardust
Her ego's been hurt, catapulted her pride, don't blame yourself.
Wither, wither, wither, dead; A flower needs energy to bloom ~
You realise it, pay Attention, don't take me for granted; respect.
Somewhere we're in multi-dimensions holding up the Love vibe.
Takes consciousness to know how to keep Love feelings flowing.
A spontaneous smile coming from the Heart ~ Beautiful essence.
Holding it up for as long as You could under the circumstances!
Awareness of these elements of HAPPINESS, of JOY, of BLISS.
Keeping them high, emotion, devotion, chemical physical desire.
All those experiences that happen when you're naturally in Love.
It's a Cosmic game, Fate's not allowing it ~ What to do? Let go
*Universes making it happen ~ of course*count y/our blessings*

Being in Love with Love.
It reminds me of my first heartbreak; Heart
ripped apart! Don't fight the tears of Love ~
See the Sacredness in it ~ tears from the heart.
With those tears wish her all the best in life.
I'm not her Lover now, you had to let her go.
Feeling the Chakra ~ Opened, Alive, be in it.
Be in that beautifully delicious bubble of Love.
From the Universal ~ surround yourself with it!
It happens to those who believe in its devoted light.
Don't focus it on any person ~ just in the Love itself.
Heart energy and the energy will send you an Angel.
Then put all your feelings into this sublime happiness.
The Core of It

*

You Keep Loving
You can't latch onto a phantom ~ not even one Memory;
You need someone to help you forget her beautiful auras.
Your endorphins are crashing all over looking for her smile.
She's met someone else, she's Happy, has a vision of her life.
Love transcending every woman ~ fuelling higher spiritual love.
Change your thoughts, get out of the gloom, sad disappointment.
If you don't want me, I'll know if she's lying when I look into her eyes.
'You Love someone set them free if they come back keep them forever'

*

Flight of light Tapestry
Should have listened to your heart not the needs of your mind.
You got what you wanted ~ Proper Shakti balance, strong Kali!
At the end of the day you gotta look after your own sanity.
Hard to take it all in ~ Your heart's beating in your mouth!
Looking for the snake in the grass ~ Everything is beautiful.

Attacked by a Buffalo
'Take Your Mind off it ~ Get another One'
"This is a Free World, get me my passport!"
*I had to break out the gate * going back to nature.*
Tuning into your essence ~ 'Je t'allumes darling...

*

Being in it
Separating ~ who gets all the pre-recorded stuff on TIVO;
½ the Labrador? Feeding on the emotions of the drama,
pulled away from the now ~ Letting it happen too.
Going with multi-dimensional flow, open to it all.
Filling it with golden light.
"I gave her the purest reflection."
You have to Love yourself otherwise it's not true ~
*The drama's not important * LOVE IS LOVE not Maya.*

*

Supersonic 'Higgs Bosun'
It's just a word but it tunes in with you.
Intuitively to Love and enjoy Peace.
Resonating it's all the same ~ One thing.
Never ending ~ faster than the speed of light.
There's a Oneness ~ Subconscious reality.
What is it that holds it all up?
*In La k'ech * Sat Chit Ananda.*

*

Confusiopoly Model of Scarcity
"I don't give a shit about your water flow ~
I want the lights to come on when I press the switch!"
As long as my cow's productive and GMO plants are growing!
All the different tangents and Illusion of choice, supporting whom?
It should all be free right now for every*being ~ completely natural.
Going to the Dubai shopping festival in diamond encrusted veiling.

Be Real * Be True
No blame, feeling peace, very deep, very high!
A lovers rejection, be in balance, pull yourself together.
I gave you the chance to let all our magic go ~
Understanding the meaning behind the words?
She took her eye off the ball, lost her attention to me.
Multi-dimensional Orgasms are very big attachments!
Letting go of all that Love, creativity and Cosmic juice.
Comes back to existence be here now ~ infinite moment
of Love ~ Allowance to be free together or deceit, defeat..

*

Proactive * Procreative
An Emotional reaction ~ Another Spiritual response.
Trusting the Universe ~ reflecting back our Love.
In one's inimitable way.
You are You ~ that's your Free choice.
Can't separate the sweetness from sugar.

*

Transmissions behind my back
Replacing our divine, luscious, blissful orgasms ~
with more orgasms from someone else, I never knew!
Ego's screaming dramas & Judgments in your false head!
Here together now, letting the Universe guide our hearts.
Why didn't you come after me if you had any feeling left?
She said she never had any time, but not avoiding me ~
In subconscious ~ multi-dimensions Life is happening
becoming ~ Regeneration ~ Singing it in to me truly.

A Chain of Rip-offs!
To face another dimension of the Sun.
Reconnect to your Inner-self
Realignment of your heart ~
No promises only to be an Open chakra.
Lotus petals vibrating softly in the breeze.
It's up to you ~ Your crystal, resonating still in tune.
Be aware of what you're wishing for ~
Manifesting your deepest desires ~ here and now.
What's more important the lure of money or the music?
Her fix ~ gotta accept it or you're always in the loss.
"You get the Gold Medal for fucking the Spirit!"

*

Love's Muse
'They Love you ~ they're not In Love with you'
"I'm losing the plot." "Cancel that one please, thank you"
I thank Heaven ~ my parents weren't big drinkers!
Don't have to go anywhere to find 'Self' ~ not Me.
You can't prance around there with a bursting Ego.
A great place to grow up. 'Love is bigger than one person'
Letting it go straight into the Heart ~ of someone you Love.

*

To my face
No respect or honesty, lowest breakdown in communication.
"I know it's very cheeky but if you are not so busy and you
would like to pass by for a smoke I would be very happy."
To make her happy and trusting in her with an open heart ~
"Why did you say cheeky?" "Because if I didn't need a smoke
I wouldn't have asked you to come." My lovely muse said!
Realisation, awareness of the changing feelings in a heart!

We're all dancing together.
"I danced in the dreaming of reality ~"
Is there anyone who doesn't like MDMA?
Bursting these bubbles that were very nice.
Clenched your face ~ no happiness in selfish.
Capt. Delicious*Beaming up a pair of lips from Orion.
*

Full Depersonalisation
You have to create a very strong wall ~
to get disconnected from that deep attachment.
Spare me that scene right now if you have any feelings.
Shapes are shifting ~ structures and dreams are melting.
Experiencing more sensitivity, no one's cleaning the trees!
To respect someone ~ to be honest with someone,
You have to be honest and respect Yourself first!
'Actions speak louder than words' Transfer of her desire.
A classical relationship at two different tangents.
Not in tune ~ Not feeling the Full Moon between us.
No shining stars shining in your eyes, no shiny auras.
Full of confusion, insecurity, fear, pain, stress, lusting,
Ego, expectations, demands, greed and blind reactions.
Another lost Drama Queen sucking the life energy out of
your open petalled Lover, leaving him dry in the muddy
wonder of being in Love ~ the perfect emotional mirage.
She took the free space and grabbed only what suited her!
That's all fine in the Universe, not in the heart of your Lover.
Now we have separated forever, you chose that without me.
Time to reflect on this, remember how much we loved to kiss.
Be conscious response, happy and true ~ I'll always Love you.
Judging from your Mind and not feeling your heart you stole away
from someone who was your most passionate Lover ~ Vive l'amour!

His side is no side

Flirting in neuro-linquistic ethnic language ~
"Let's fuck to the end of the Divine rainbow!"
Mind Control ~ fulfilling dark and secret needs.
'Who to contact in case of Emergencies?'
"The relevant deity for the region"
With Consciousness comes Awareness.

*

Fractal Symmetry

The Model for Transhuman builders is commerce, to make a profit!
Piss scared, I love magic more than Politics, how about LSD?
Perceiving or not perceiving it ~ Ancient forests full of Timelessness.
Shakti's Vortex, voluptuous curves spinning my dynamo turbine!
"The hotter she is the more space between her molecules"
'Nothing to Fear except Fear Itself' who screamed that?
'You make your bed now you have to lie in it without me'
Water's meandering patterns ~ carving existential channels.
The banks holding the stream? You can taste the difference
from out of a mountain river or out of a tap in Birmingham!
Cosmic Nature as a whole which we are all part of ~

*

Fear of Kali

Keeping an Open mind ~ Infinity is a concept going nowhere soon.
No words to describe what is actually real * Life is Everywhere.
Bottom of the class in Science, I didn't even dissect a frog!
He's trapped banging things together and blowing them up!
Once it's blown up it's gone ~ dematerialised into Space

Beautiful memories ~ Learning to become the Observer
*I'm saying all this with a Smile in my heart ~ no games. I've been
hoping for this opening reconnection one day for y/our realization
of the deep love that we felt for each other to be truly recognized ~
Thank you for sharing your feelings with me which I always believed
in too. It wasn't just my passion, infatuation, attachment, a dream of
Psychedelia! It is a healing for my spirit to know that you feel the
same. I know I saw that light sparkling in your eyes. I never had a
doubt then you left me in such loss and pain that my crystal smashed
to pieces and I wondered if I'd ever see you again! Was it just Egoic,
delusion, an ecstatic state of romance, a magic trance to deceive 'me'
or did we really look into each other's heart and dance? I did my best
to hold your soul but you flew on your journey where I was not invited.
I asked the Universe if true for directions to a Higher Consciousness
Unconditional Love, letting you go or was it just my Complete Illusion?
I can't get my head around that one even tho' it seems to make a lot
of sense, it doesn't seem right It's a concept that has become the core
of Eastern philosophies ~ and hard to argue it! Yet I would more likely
say avoid sadness and disappointment by expecting everything from
everyone but these are all projections of the mind to protect us; Fair
enough. BUT as an overall view it's putting limits on life that hasn't
happened and so won't happen. It's another Control mechanism. It's
EXCELLENT to keep it in our minds as a GUIDE but not to put up a
Mental wall because that is stopping new experience. "She deliberately
and completely avoided you because she knew that you still Loved her!"
'It is better to have Loved and lost than to have never Loved' That's not
true because we never lose! Whatever we experience with an open heart
is the Ultimate even though we might end up in the darkness because of
our 'Expectations'. We always have to be more Open than Life itself in
us to get the full Realisation and also we enter into Sharing the human
*Adventure of Nature on Earth*and in Cosmic*OMNI*PRESENCE**

Cleopatra's best mate ~ Oxytocin

Dragging them off to Paradise ~ Seeing some clear blue Sky.
'It is what it is' & it isn't any different is it; Right delusional?
"I can heal anything because I don't give a fuck anymore!"
That's not real is it? Couldn't you simply just be Truly you?
Another muse, femme fatale crushed my balls because her
own ego didn't get its dreams fulfilled and she broke down!
Doesn't know any more. This is her truth destroying her open
Troubadour lover's supersensitive soul ~ that you once adored!
Sharing in the bliss and beauty sucking in Cherry Love energy.
The Ecstasy oasis is now parched, her spirit takes flight in fright.
"What the f... was that, didn't see that one coming Baby;
Really Deep!" Out of the darkness, Storms have reappeared!
A Heart grenade smashed me into Devastation's sad despair.
Inside the cage of your Mind - A Gulag, Concentration camp.
To have loved and lost ~ Lost nothing * It's All Love Potential!
You've made this cruel disconnection now we're Separated
in the 3rd dimensional ~ Is this really love's free flow?
You thought I was your problem now you've found
a bigger one, your Ego's Karma drama panorama!
"Gone off the Universal edge * I'm not on Atlantis!"
What the f... do you want from me, do you know?
A non telepathic heart asking for my Unconditional love ~
Betrayed all the trusting and creativity darling of our dream.
Surrender let it go ~ let it glow in the Cosmic energetic stream.

*

Death is happening * Vivre la Honey Bee

Flamboyant & Thoughtless; they're good when they get you crying!
Everything happening in the moment ~ Now is the Truth.
We're always at the Point of No Return ~
Don't know what they've resurrected!
Happy & Hard ~ It's a Magic name.

"I want to look into your deep blue eyes!"
Love and Light downpour ~ erotic taboo rainbows.
Licking full passion, melting on my Goddess' lips.
Penetration deep into her steaming wet rain forest.
I want to seduce your hard throbbing nipples
I want to suck your honey sweet sensual clit.
I want to touch the fire in your gorgeous arse ~
I want to kiss your erogenous nymphs from Venus
dancing on the tip of your wild ~ delirious tongue.
I want to cum inside you like two exploding stars.
I want to feel you sliding up my hard cock in ecstasy,
screaming, unbridled in never ending exquisite rapture.
I want to hold your true love tightly in my arms.
I want to taste & smell your Multi*orgasmasms.
You aren't going anywhere and I want to be
forever inside you in such beautiful bliss.
Letting our love reunite ~ reignite in us!
Your open heart has declared its love for me
I want to ravish your sublime, dripping pussy,
devour it as a delicious Sicilian cheesecake.
My fingers pressing into your sacred Temple,
my body's desire to caress Its burning flame.
I want to embrace your free spirit ~ with mine.
I want to lie beside you in Heaven's tranquility
My magma flowing into your Oceanic ~ Divine

*

Direct from the Tea garden to Tea pot
No more Gangster Islam "You look like you've come from Wakilstan!"
God comes to You with his music ~Triphop it's not Yours!
"I haven't had that pain since I started the Ayuhuasca diet"
Many people are living inhumanely Mr. Sociopath Sir!
"We gotta get rid of corrupt, ignorant, violent Politics"

'L'Amour de l'Ocean Poetique'

Love fully Rejected! "I went through a Painful Hell for you/us/me."
Give her the respect for being honest and go have detached sex;
Not conning someone, playing with your life as the cuckold Fool.
I won't respect myself; Why do you want to be in bed with someone
who wants to voraciously suck someone else not you? It's her Ego's
pleasure, sexual gratification that blanks her from feeling anything
for you, the slightest sensitivity when she is only caring about her
own desires. Shock! You absolutely don't exist anymore in her life ~
Sad, Unbelievable ~ call it Selfish but I still can't accept it is Real!
Not again, be honest don't say you Love me unless it's true; Why?
Give your energy to a woman who wants you, filling you with Shakti

*

Soul not Soul

Psycho-manic Neurotic ~ "We're too erotic for War"
Big brother went to fight, the men never came back! KIA!
Hallo I am the Public, beyond the law! Dirty bitch she's no Angel.
Full Power Ego tripping, only 'Me' no feelings of happiness for me.
'She dumped you so she's the winner not as the loser ~ No excuses!'
At her mercy, don't let your emotions take charge, drives you Insane.
At least don't get involved now she's being fucked by another man.
Wrong wo/man brings wrong energy, she won't suffer you will!
Who's been an asshole to have believed in it because you
desperately wanted to feel in absolute Love ~ Joyful kisses.
"Ego blocked her, took over her Mind and she's loving it!"
The Ego/Love movie will continue the actors will change ~
You Love being in Love, only way to get all that Bliss back.
She's left Love now she's reflecting Negativity, pain to you.
Maya ~ Love it's Not yours or hers, leave it and you lose it!
Peace of Mind ~ really the thing that money can't buy * Love.

89

Surreal Hippie & Alien Jam

Torture it ~ just a bit! Stop with her auto Psy-eroticism!
Why she left you for someone else and never told you ~
She was getting fucked somewhere by someone new!
A very nice and easy changing of emotional energy*space for her.
She won't accept the truth of her selfish, deceitful actions; In denial!
Isn't that what you always wanted? Accepting insanity as normal.
Realising makes you sane. You can't look at others only be yourself.
In the moment ~ 'to be or not to be' * Open-Spatial Awareness.
In the dream there is something real ^ Why deconstruct people?
Forgiveness ~ Acceptance the only thing to FREE your mind.
"All the World is a stage and we are merely players ~"
"You give me that pain, thanks!" 'Everyone's a fool for love'
Universal is a Mental-concept*nothing is really good or bad.
It's happening in the moment ~ Observing it, you're seeing it
from outside the Prison of your Mind ~ In SPACE * looking in!
Natural vibration brought you to me never a possession by Force ~
Absolutely Unacceptable, realise who is responsible for this today!
People in Power of course; No excuses but Full existential ignorance,
selfish inhuman condition; Crimes against Humanity still exist on Earth!

*

Heavenly Grace

Whatever happened to you? Possessed by a sexy Apsara nymph!
'Be Aware of what you're wishing for' ~ Bottom Ocean feeders.
In the end You showed me your black heart, who you were.
No light, no feelings, no consciousness, fully ignorant Ego!
Her Self-destruct hormones, not Trusting, killing my Spirit.
Emotions wading through a deep depression in the desert.
No Star fields, no Oasis, no true heart to guide a traveler.
Shiva Valley all night trance ~ "We got the Chemicals!"

Betrayal of a Partner in Soul
When they go through something really, really, really deep.
Knowing they have to reflect themselves in you*the Effects.
A finger in the wound she's trying to hide all of her emotions.
Going to a Higher LOVE Level to rise from the last lost Love!
Knowing that nothing that is True will ever be lost because ~
it's only an Illusion, be thankful what you have lived through it.
Give it away you'll never understand the causes of this tragedy!
Knowing that everything is temporary ~ ever changing, even you Baby!
Give yourself some Space, some Silence in the Stillness of your Souls.
Don't take it so Personally * Seriously ~ go and have a lovely walk..

*

Given absolutely no other choice!
I've been holding on to this Image that I couldn't ever let go ~
Too precious, couldn't imagine letting contentment flow ~ off!
I like it, I Love it, I Want to keep it, never wanna lose that vibe!
Full on Passionate Addiction, squirt me another endorphin fix ~
from your delicious, lascivious, Spirit's mix of intoxicating delights,
hot desires and raging fires for 'My Mind' to conjure up and create.
But it's all been a very beautiful and tragic Super delusional dream.
Next one is different ~ I seem to be in another place on this Spiral.
You have to let it go because there's NOTHING left to hold onto but
her memory. There comes that moment in time ~ its changed, Gone!
Have to let her go, she's fucked off. Holding on is all she's left you at
most! It's impossible to carry on. Change has unnaturally come to set
me, to set us free, to be at peace, releasing the addiction and finding
a new reality of higher consciousness & Unconditional Love Space!
Great now take it easy, get the senses back, try tuning into your heart.

Quick Sand Negativities Sinking Into Depression Lake

She's cut all the Love bonds for reasons that I never knew ~
Now I know why she has absolutely No Love feeling for me!
Wow, we had such blissful intimacies, now just disappeared.
"Let's be friends" I've heard that sad old refrain lots before ~
She needed me to give her something that I could never fulfill.
Couldn't make her dreams come true so banished me into Limboo!
I've discovered the secret lines you followed ~ Now it ALL Is Clear!
Crossing personality borders into another behavioral World by grace.

*

In My Skull

Mistrust*Misunderstanding*Miscommunication*Missing feeling.
Have some Pink powder never be the same again ~ Never is!
But it reflected that Negativity into a True Reality and we
made Space to fall into and test Our emotions of Devotion.
Do you know what you are doing, what you are telling me
to do and what you want me to accept as your Once lover?
Do you realise, are you aware, do you even care anymore ~
this lovely flower is dying from neglect, what did you expect?
You threw me back into the Ocean ~ swim or drown it's up to you.
'It is what it is' ~ Can't do out more! The shock and grief, the loss,
the sad disappointment, the grieving collapsing heart & numb brain,
this unbelievable new Ireality! "She's involved with someone else!"
"She's Involved with Someone else!" "Involved with Someone else!"
What is that, please explain! Could you foresee the consequences
of this on a sensual Open Spirit? You're well and truly fucked now ~
Psychedelic Buddhist hippie! Remember it's all an Illusion, Oh Yeah!
Super Spiritual don't yu know? Can you please sing me a lullaby Baby?

Reality Caravanserai
You need some form of light in the Centre of the sacred Yoni.
Keep away from me with Your fear and Selfish confusion ~
After a year of running away from me for your own pleasure.
My complete rejection & denial, you needing to love the next.
Dumped me paralysed in Space, let me drown in memories.
"Now only come to me with smiles & love ~ not selfish shame.
Feelings in your heart you share fully with me not hidden guilt."
Any Understanding, It's beyond comprehension,
just be here now in the Magic ~ together or not!
What are you really saying you want to give
and what are you truly wanting from me?
I remember your joy the first days we met.
Look in the mirror and ask yourself....
Why would I hate you?

*

Hot Bodies * Beings Together
Disappointment from an Anticipation of being in between your thighs.
You're free to do what you want obviously you're not my Possession!
But wouldn't you have enjoyed spending a night with me in Ecstasy?
*Having that delightful experience making Love on MDMA's * Fantasy!*
You didn't feel the fires of desire, hot motivations, flames of Passion
or any interest to come home to me until after dawn?
Free ~ Doing what you want and you chose not to.
"Wherever is the Silence is the Love"
You knew I wanted to be with you!
Am I Being taken for a fool?

Ask A Question

Who wants to reminisce ~ momentarily? I crashed through Lalaland
to you! A flawless diamond, Perfection ~ being in each moment Now.
"When did you know that you had fallen out of Love with me again?"
No guilt feeling; She's stopping to think about it and gives no reply ~
"Have you fallen out of Love with me?" I didn't realize she hasn't been
in Love with me for a long time but she behaved as if she was to me!
Surprise that's a Big change in our relationship and I didn't even know
except for the lack of passion and any sort of caresses ~ that's not just
her 'bad day trip' that's the End of a beautiful Love affair! Her choice!
And it happened months ago and she still didn't tell me what she felt.
"I don't know if I love you or I don't Love you ~ how do I know?"
You certainly know that you Loved me & that we were on a super sexy
rocket of desires going to the stars and exploding in Cosmic galaxies!
We were together crossing the Universe, entwined in our hearts; Yet
*somehow she bailed out, wasn't enough * multi orgasms in her auras.*
You Loved me completely, now you don't know ~ You don't Love me!
That's a seismic shift for me to allow, to get my Consciousness around
that one. Drugged up with psychotropic Mind-Form-Altering chemicals.
Acid, MDMA, couple of chillums on this Magic aphrodisiac Island with
a giant Priapus lingham next to your naked flesh and you fall asleep!
No intimacies, no kiss, nout, with her back to me; It's gone, not there.
That bright sensational desire in your eyes & thighs has disappeared.
That gorgeous smile ~ your delicious hot, soaking wet pussy's left me.
You are happy, new dreaming and I'm wanting to Love you as before.
It's died, gone away forever ~ And I'm staring at an Arse to die for!

"I thought you dumped me ~ You thought what you wanted to"
Because you realised you deserved to be dumped, ~ WHY?
Very precious; Your reflection gave me a lot of Pain Baby!
Programmed Identification * Structural addiction patterning.
I can't f...... let it go, a Manic-obsessive inside my head or so
I must believe it to be true, going crazy after my dreams of you!
Believe in what you believe, in this perception there's no hope!
Life will do those sorts of things to you to Realise its meaning.
Come back to your TRUSTING HEART in any relationship ~
In Real Space to feel the Invisible Love is true for me & you.
"Please forgive me darling for giving you any pain or fear."
You have absolutely nothing to feel blame or guilt about.
'Don't need to look for grief ~ grief finds you soon enough!'

*

You fell out of Love with me NOT for having to leave you Now but
because I was separated from you before! I thought it was all fine ~
You told me that and I hadn't any idea. You didn't tell me otherwise.
Would you invite me home so full of passion for you my Love, to lie
beside you but for my Love to be rejected as before. I never made the
link that you had fallen out of Love even tho' you showed no desires!
There was some other reason, this realization too incomprehensible!
Your JOY stopped flowing without my knowing but you did and didn't
tell me ~ You made me feel scared of upsetting you by touching you.
Another stepping stone of Love on Life's journey ~ Thank you Baby.
I will really miss You and what we created together, such happy bliss!
"Could it ever come back could she Love me again once she's let go?"
Thank You for making my life beautiful, all the more amazing in Goa.
All those magical memories ~ living in the moment * being here now.

Golden Wings

I am so happy to get such a letter from you, I've waited a long
time for this awareness to appear and naturally express itself.
The feelings I always had in my Heart for you are still alive.
I Never Stopped Loving you ~ the love we shared is Magical.
I told you many times that in my experience it is Rare to have such
DEEP feelings. I still love you of course. I never switched you Off ~
as I always believed that what we surrendered to each other was our
Purest love. I'm very very happy that finally you came to realise, not
deny this true bliss we enjoyed that made our hearts and spirits smile
and fly with so much happiness and that this is the wonderful light
guiding our lives. Is this the big lesson we've learnt? A Real Love or
a madly delusional Passion poem? Not to be negative or cynical in
this crazy world of our mind's attachments, of infatuation and ego's
desperate illusions and fears ~ but harmoniousness within such deep
connecting, trusting eyes. I entered this experience with you to Know
these BEAUTIFUL sensations, feelings between a man & a woman,
diving to the core. You gave me everything, that's why it still touches
our Souls' Space ~ On the other side that love as you know well can
be extremely painful because I allowed myself to be so open with you.
I tried to hold the balance but I decided to jump over the edge ~ with
You and to Trust in the Universe * that was my choice. I do not regret it
but I paid a heavy price of despair when you left me in the way you did.
I know the Real suffering you had; Now I don't know anything of your life!
Are you still in your relationship, it sounds like you have this connection,
you've made that vital choice for yourself? I cannot love you in that
way if you're with another. I'm free, y/our love lifts me to the light ~
I'm saying all of this with a Smile in my heart ~ no hidden Ego games.
After my loss of you I've been hoping for a reconnection one day for
Y/our Realisation of the deep Love that we felt for each other to be
truly recognised. Thank you for sharing your feelings with me which I
always kept believing in too. It wasn't just my illusion, passion, desire,

96

infatuation, mad Attachment, LSD dream, it was Real! Was it Yours?
It's a healing for my Spirit to know that you feel the same. I know I
saw that light sparkling in your eyes & I know inside ~ Your smile
kissed my lips with your love as I kissed yours ** I never had any
doubt then you dumped me without a word in such loss and pain!
My Heart smashed to pieces, I wondered if I'd ever see you again!
Was it just our delusion, an ecstatic state of trance, magical romance
to deceive 'me' or did we really look into each other's true Souls and
dance? I did my utmost to hold your Spirit but you flew on your own
journey with someone new where I was not wanted. Am I insane for
holding onto a ghost? I asked the Universe if it's true for directions to
Higher Consciousness * Unconditional Love or was it all Pure Illusion?

*

Paseo de las Delicias
You Are the King & the Queen
Are you happy? Yes Happy to be alive.
Tell me what do you see? I see the Truth.
Changing vibrations at the Jardines de Paradas.
Tranquillo growing into a perfect angel
At an Oasis for my Spirit

*

On Dream Street
Welcome on board the Milky Way Federation's Blue Meteorite crew.
I found people in the right bubble, had some beautiful Sunrises in life.
Just another virtual Mind Psy*Track detour try Gy*Psy trance
Everything has an Expiry date ~ he's not as dumb as he looks!
'Best Before, Sell By, Finished, Throw it in the skip, Collateral damage!'
You've come a long way Baba no need to go back there * the Palaces &
slave, concubine harems. "It's about having feelings of empathy, stupid!"
"It's a little Oasis here"

Different Plastic Priorities
Do you recognize ~ that your feelings to me have changed or not?
We were like two exploding volcanoes erupting in full thermal flow!
Now we've cooled. Can't you see, different feelings, it's so obvious?
You chose what to do with your Freedom when you left me tripping,
when you didn't have enough intent or the slightest sense ~
to spend it making Love with me ~ forget the consequences.
You came home tired after dawn and fell asleep. Is It the End?
OK then let the attachment to the Object of desire go ~
"I feel your resistance to me; Why?" 'Keep It Real Baby!'
"You said at the beginning that I would break your heart"
"I never said to you that you would make me break mine first!"
Stepping back from my involvement ~ what does that portend?
*Life Is Sacred * Innocence Is Bliss*

*

The subtlest Maya playing with our Minds and Hearts ~
Our Utopias, our Oblivions, our Ecstasies and Sufferings,
our Blisses in your Kisses, our devastations with your loss.
How to go to the essence of this mirage and to be released?
*To be free from the Avatar holding us in its duality, You * Me.*
To feel and know the promise I made to the Divine Goddess ~
That was then and this is now and I moved on and I Am Happy.
It's just a captivating Illusion darling and to wish you 'Adieu'

*

A Demon Lost in Disguise
*Beheaded by Venus * Executed in Public to satisfy her Painful Soul!*
So ruthless made her own happy dream memory as if I never existed!
In flames of deceit to the Unreal, no gratitude for your Light worker ~
The kiss of betrayal, a traitor in the garden conjuring her own fantasy.
Looking deep into my eyes, picking up the pieces of burning wreckage
without any empathy, not accepting any responsibility; You don't exist
*anymore in that hallucinatory * emotional, fierce Capricorn Jet stream.*

Love Is Conscious

Your last message about the love we shared was amazing and true
and when I said 'Thank You' I meant it because you finally got it
together enough to recognise what we Shared and what I did for you.
It sounded so beautiful and you captured all the Magic, you also
realised some of your own behaviour. I had waited a very long time
for you to do this. You put a lot of intelligent thought, Soul and
feeling into it.. You were being honest. It was a wonderful way to
clear things up and move on with only positive memories. I got all
of that! When you first walked into my life you said two things were
important, Honesty and respect. You also said that you had a very big
lesson to learn from being with me & that I would break your heart!
(Which I would never do). The fact that you could write such a letter
showed that the dream we created, I had successfully kept it intact so
You suffered No psychological or emotional scarring from me in this
Separation and you would feel ok to eventually reflect this ~
not going into some dark hole of guilt, anger or resentment!

Your letter was a sweet poem I loved it but you missed out one chapter
and I hope it's not the final chapter. This is one that only I could write
and so I send it to you now to give another aspect to the one you have.
We both agree with this Amazing Love we shared and how deep it was.
When it goes so deep because we opened ourselves up so fully to each
other through trust & respect then when that 'changes' there are
obviously going to be powerful Consequences, as we know!

I wrote a few letters to you about what I was feeling and at the same time
I was trying everything to still hold up these feelings of love & light not
letting them just disappear forever! I wanted to be there for you and
to always help you get through your Hell; Which I have done!
This is how I try to live my life and to be conscious,
aware and love unconditionally not just for 'ME'

I wrote these letters not with the intention of sending them to you but for my own healing. Also to be honest and not just let you believe that I was able to come through this with no suffering! My love for you was so full & spiritual but also with the deepest Sensitivity of a Man in passionate love with a woman. I have absolutely no regrets for having shared this with you ~You know that.

*

<u>*I'm happy now to finally get your message and to finish my healing!*</u> *If you have any respect left for me and you still honour the love that we had and why wouldn't you, here is a letter about my feelings of how I felt about our separation. I wrote it a while ago to help me to come to terms with things and to exorcise this pain and negativity I had because I was holding up a big lie and I needed to confront it. I hope it helps You to understand the complex feelings that exist in Love at the extremely sensitive levels that existed between me and you and we can both move ~ forward. I didn't write it to blame you, what good does that do for me now it only makes for bitterness (and I take my responsibility in this too and hope you forgive me) but to try to show the 'Negative curse' & to realise that I cannot hold up any light of truth in a 'Higher' relationship I'd hoped to have, with it still unspoken. They are Observations & I hope you read this as an insight into your behavioral patterns at the deepest level of your feelings which can only come from someone who shared in them with you. Hopefully you'll learn something about parts of yourself; How your denial, rejection & negative behaviour effects people who only wanted to love you! Don't take this as a personal Attack it's not! What had I done to cause you to behave in such an angry, negative & resentful way making excuses? This is me you're treating like this, the person who you say you loved and opened up your Heart to? Ok so you went off, changed me/us for another lifestyle! I stepped back made it easy, never interfered (I was given no other choice and its suddenness was a Devastating SHOCK!) except to want to keep in*

touch please! Is this really the great lesson you came to learn from me? Is this what Y/our * Love finally turns into Baby! Is it what you truly mean when you say, 'I'm the Only one that knows who you are'

Conscious ~ Honesty & Respect of Love/r

From the start of this letter I want you to keep in mind everything I did for you. You most probably wouldn't have the life you have now in Goa happy with your children if it wasn't for me. I don't say this to make you guilty but to make you remember that I was always there for you yet you ended up treating me in the worst way possible by leaving me for someone else and not even telling me for over several months whilst I thought I was giving you Space to realise what we had as you knew it to be true. Yet you dumped me, you betrayed me, our sacred trust, you lied, were deceitful and your anger and selfish ego allowed a relationship to develop behind my back. You will never admit this, so far you have denied the truth of this and given me some simple, stupid reasoning why it happened. You treated me as an Idiot(action) because you had lost all respect and honesty. I gave you this free Space to express yourself, yet you still played this Negative game. I allowed you to speak to me, to behave with me in such a horrible way, to see who you were & what you understood, what you were conscious of and cared for!

(Asking me to leave you at 11pm each night with the relationship we'd had was such a f.... horrible emotional experience for me but I put up with it not wanting to piss you off & cause you to react in such dismissive ways! The scenes by S. valley beach were the most terrible abuse for treating me as a real Nobody because you selectedly had changed your 'lifestyle' and in your letter you have no memories of any of this it seems and when you asked me to come round for a smoke because 'You had nothing to smoke!' That's a Mental haze! What the fuck, are you conscious of any of this and how it's affected

101

me, a Lover in your life!? You can see this also as a Control pattern to get your own way depending who the person is in the dynamic and I also allowed this to try and hold onto you & what we meant together.

I put myself in this same sad situation when you left me, trying to hold you somehow, not wanting to lose you but as you've admitted this abuse has happened so why pretend it was all Roses. I'm now Releasing myself from the promise I made to myself to always be there for you as a Light worker because you're still unaware of my suffering which came out of being in love with you and you saying the same to me. This allows me to also let you go on that level & so be free in my life accepting the Reality that you chose a 'new lifestyle' You can blame me and say it was my 'detachment' with your children too but that's something I tried to explain the day you walked into my life. I did my best & never lied but you cut me out of that too. This is not to blame you but to inform you of Consequences to someone you say in your last letter meant so much to you but in reality aren't they just lovely words and you have no other understanding? You said I helped you find what you were looking for in Life for it to be complete but it was totally dishonest. You say you needed me or you would have fallen apart but where was the empathy for me; only complete denial!? What effect do you think that might have on me, is this the way you respond to your ~ 'Light worker?' It's taking the piss, can I accept you couldn't do anything else? I forgive you but I want you to realise this!

You want me to make a copy of your book which was the highlight of the magical expression of our love whilst you have treated me, this person who always was there for you, who always wanted to carry on this love with you, in the most despicable way. Obviously this pattern of behaviour you understood as 'normal reactions!' How did I continue with it, this negativity, anger, emotional abuse & aggression? I have seen it all before and I can understand it! You ultimately have the right to do what you want but we had a relationship of deep trust that normally is to be treated carefully or there is deep pain and suffering.

*Basic stuff but you didn't care at all because you were overcome
by only ~ what you wanted. You cared nothing for me &
yet were happy to enjoy my energy when it suited you!*

*

*I went through a Nightmare to continue to keep this connection of us
together & that is fine but you still have no appreciation of your actions.
I am writing this letter because I cannot continue holding up the light
when you still won't recognize your duplicitous behavior to me.
Now I have finally received the clearer picture of what happened
even if you can't see or admit it. How your subconscious' Karma &
desires were affecting your behavior. How your insecure mind was
madly 'scheming to get what you wanted without any thought for me!'
Why me? Because I was still in your life as a person who deserved
some truth & respect. Don't put me in a pattern of those others
close to you, who have wronged you and whom you despise!*

*You changed completely in December since you went to work
and spent all your time ~ with a man who you already knew well
and by then you had basically denied me/us in your life, you had
your own agenda going on and I didn't fit into it because you allowed
yourself to disconnect from me for your own reasons. I saw you once
a week and you didn't seem to realise what was happening to us, at
least so I thought. You kept saying you were too tired and busy with
school and kids; I believed you and gave you that trusting Space ~*

*

*Yes now I understand why you had all these bad moods with me for
no apparent reason but you kept your Feelings Secret from me and
allowed me to continue to believe in our relationship and to go through
another two months believing in you/us, in our truth and respect ~ but
you had already broken that sacred bond. You said I'm maybe the one
who understands you best! Yes I do I see your highs & lows. You say
I care when you sent me your messages to your sister. Yes I do; but*

now I experienced the negative energy that you have, I never saw that one coming at all Baby! I always held the Spiritual light up for you/us, Love Consciousness of ecstatic states & their changing ~ When the Lover is dumped at that depth in such a way it's a long journey back to Heal a Heart & Spirit! By expressing this I can heal this 'poisoning' in my heart, from this Disbelief that someone who I loved, who knew how much I felt for them could behave in such a selfish, cruel, arrogant & ignorant way! You even seemed to enjoy it when I finally found out 'that you were involved with someone' ~ you got a thrill seeing me in despair and pain, you wanted to hurt me for some reason as a sign of your own powerful, egoist-Self. This is another common pattern and you behaved in such a low way yet in your delusion you say you were always thinking of me!

*

How could you have been, how is it possible? It was all so easy for you! I tell you with no malice but great disappointment & sadness that such a beautiful love relationship could degenerate into such nasty bullshit. You do not realise what you/we had, to destroy it in that way. I don't let lovers in my life go easy but I am releasing myself from the bonds we have ~ I can't pretend by sending you a copy of this book that you are the same person. Why do you even ask me for it? Do you have no sense of insulting my feelings again? Are you so naive, so self- centred, so blind, thinking that you can throw anything at me and as I'm open hearted and trying to practice Love that I will put up with it all! Is this how you respond to my feelings of Love by abusing them? See what reactions develop what satisfaction you get! I cannot pretend this is cool, it is a full dishonour of what we had because you destroyed that/us/me in such a bad way and because you won't admit it or take responsibility for your actions; Who cares! It took me this long to realise some of your behavioural patterns!

*As I say, I was the person who stood by you I gave you all my Love ~
I always told you that yet you've purposely killed it and left me terrible
mental-emotions to deal with that you were fully Unconscious of or not!
Why do that to me the one who was always there for you? You say that
you don't know how I feel that's because you didn't give a fuck about
how I feel, you switched it off! That one night you saw me at the bar
with a girl I know how much of a shock that was even though you'd
kept saying it was over and yet it never was! You know how painful
that was, you had those feelings, you are not so insensitive! So try
& imagine if you will how it was for me but 100 times more painful
because your affair went on behind my back for over two months!
You just said, "I would have broken you if you hadn't got me back"*

*I saw your pain then and I would never do that because I felt the pain
too and I knew what the consequences would be for you if I left you!
I couldn't do it anyway because I loved you. You saw, witnessed also
your friend going crazy with her breakup did you Not realise that I was
Devastated too; would it have made any difference to your disdain?
From December it was certainly happening even if you won't admit it!
It was never right then (Xmas & New Year's Eve!!!) and that's why in
January, Intuitively I had to make my 'cry from the heart' to seriously
ask you what was happening by walking away & giving you time to
Realise * 'If you don't give the flower water it will wither and die ~'
A simple truth!*
*

*Normally we might have come back together I hoped to but because
of this other relationship happening it was such an easy way out for
you to walk away with no responsibility, remorse, pain or Awareness
and stay away for over two months without a word to me by way of
explanation and thinking, 'Fuck him then!' You say you thought I had
dumped you that is absolute bullshit you made no effort, never were
really interested to even ask me what was happening even though it*

was clear as you'd chosen to go already! Easy for you to do in this extreme and so Selfish. You dumped me in such a horrible way, it's never nice and was not helped in any way by you in fact the opposite like treating me as if I never existed! Did I really mean so little to you even though you keep saying I did so much to Open you and I know that I did! It seems you can't accept that truth and so come up with simplified versions of events and so I tried to work with that reality! Why bother? Because such experiences together mean something! You say, 'go with the flow' that's fine too but treat people properly not like shit! Why do that anyway to a caring person such as me ~ in your life, what did I do to hurt you so much, to bring such anger into your heart? OK it was tough but not to end it behind my back; avoiding me like that, we live in the same village with same friends! I can't go on pretending this never happened it is too painful for Me and I have to make this clear because you are in denial and don't really give a fuck because you've moved on to the next better thing and 'It is as it is!' ~ It's impossible that you are Unconscious about this even though you behave like nothing really happened, it's not a big deal! Well Dearest you need to have More * empathy in this world of human relationships! OK you can say 'well fuck him and forget it' that's the easy way. It doesn't alleviate the pain I've had because of your deception, unfaithfulness, betrayal, rejections over that time but it helps me to finally make it clear to you my darling and allow this truth to heal my heart! A friend finally told me when I asked about you; "She's involved with someone else, didn't you know?"

*

Remember I am not blaming you I am sharing an expression of the experience I had with you. As you did I am giving it closure! You may be unaware of these things when in stress and anger, not satisfied with your expectations, needs, until you get it fulfilled; 'Whatever the situation, where is the appearance of Love' looking for someone else. It's all Our own Ego trip, human reaction, our emotional, impulsive ~

instinctive drive. When getting what you need you are wonderful like all of us and Being aware of this! When depressed, someone criticizes you there is an immediate negative reaction ~ self-defensive which is a Power trip to Control the situation & have the will to say, 'fuck you then!' to those who love you but 'criticised you'. It seems I have to try to accept this crazy situation or lose you ~ even though later there may be regrets! Relationship patterns! It made me scared to be so candid for Fear of losing what I most wanted to keep, You! You were my beautiful muse, my Lover, my Smiling, creative spirit geisha. Shit appears to happen, conditioned like this all the time you might think from seeing others ~ these doubtful projections seem to be the way these relationships end!

*

But it isn't like that for me, in the world that I live in, the world that you say you understood, loved & was truly inspired by. There's full forgiveness and understanding but saying such things to my face as, "I wouldn't have asked you here if I didn't need a smoke." Ego-reaction, resentment; Rejecting everything is tough even for me from the lips of such a love! I say this with true feeling not to fuck you up but to share these feelings that I've been going through for a long time now. As you say I gave you your freedom to live again! I wouldn't have done it in that way if I'd known the truth of what had been happening. I did give you Space to think about us out of my deepest love but I didn't realize how I would be repaid! Your feelings were dreaming somewhere else! You never said what was going on even when you were confused, distraught; Secrets you chose not to reveal nor to be honest with me & there are Consequences in this Real world of human, Love feelings! Completely denying my existence as if we hadn't any Heart between us, fully rejecting me down on the beach! You've forgotten this ignorance for someone who shared such an Amazing love relationship with you? Is there any respect for me, for the Love poems that you wrote in this beautiful book for me and from your truly knowing that there are only a very few people in your life who have always been there ~ so much for you? If you can throw that/me in the rubbish in such a way and then carry on in life like that, then don't pretend in higher ideals, it's egotistic bullshit, just what You want and I'm sure you can see a prior pattern. If you want to communicate in the future in some way then as your first words to me were ~ 'with Respect and honesty.' Where was it? This dream you have of being in Spirit, being truly Conscious depends on our honest, unselfish actions not just on easy words, excuses & emotional Reactions done to get Control. 'Untruths' happened so I can't continue to give you this higher energy ~ inspiration as if nothing ever happened because I/we are frightened to acknowledge what really went on, this nasty ending of our relationship, our open intimacy in our being together as One & carry on pretending it's all fine because of memories ~ that once existed in these beautiful words of the Goddess, of true love alive in feelings deep in y/our heart. What went so so wrong to change that? It changed for you and it was never the same since I had to leave but especially since my return to be with you in August. You never gave me/us a chance. You were in a big stress, running away from me all the time. I found reasons why and I did everything to hold our Love up but it did nothing for you and it finally made me so unhappy too. Yet you said you loved me, that you always were thinking of me that it was too painful yet you did nothing to bring that love back! Why?

*

I try to be a Light worker. I am someone who you will always Love because I gave you back meaning in your life and Opened up and freed your heart to love. You keep saying this but in practice you did Nothing to keep it alive only continuing in Fears, doubt & negativity. Yet I carried on with the belief that you would come back to me ~ How could you give up such an Amazing Connection like we had? But you did & you just kept on with the empty words and I carried on hoping your love feelings were still there. Now is a new journey, think about it, look in the mirror and realise your behaviour and of

108

your actions on someone who had very deep love & trust feelings*
energy bonding with you & Psyche * emotional * causes * effects.
Messages of a Light worker aren't just nice words > Consequences*
'It is as it is' ~ Love Is Consciousness

*

My Movie's called....

'Cosmic Memory' ended differently! The Rocket on a mission of Love
to Venus went off course and was blown up, out of control heading
into the Sun. Without any word the Co-pilot had defected to another
Planet where she got her dream, a new lifestyle as a secure, happy
woman; Still in eternal devotion but "She's lost Love's frequency!
Keeping her own beautiful selective memory ~ but it's "Goodbye!"

*

The Captain of the ship was lost somewhere out in deepest Space *
Devastated ~ floating through a black hole in full Shock & Awe and
Amazing disbelief, still wondering what the fuck had Really happened!
He never betrayed his promise ~ Tuning in his radiant powers sending
Sun * Light * beams across her Milky way. * Oblivious to his destiny
She dreams and writes romantic poetry... So here's a few for you ~

Loving the Ultimate Syndrome ~ Reflections Flowing

'The Damsel in Distress & The Knight in Light * Amour Affair'
Setting up a Psyche*logical, emotional, Spiritual love pattern.
She says, "I know you will break my heart" on our first date!
I've made a sacred vow a long time ago to uphold the Love ~
truth, righteousness of the dhamma, chivalry of a man's heart
and not to underestimate the consequences of y/our romantic
adventures on y/our karma, destiny, revelation, sacred Spirit ~
Being a Light worker under the Tree of Life, letting it go ~ Ego;
'Me' ~ you, mundane life, World, in order to find Understanding.
Free to be in peace with my heart & mind ~ here & now happy!

The subtlest Maya playing with our Minds & deepest feelings,
our Open Utopias, our Oblivions, our ecstasies & sufferings,
our blisses in y/our kisses our devastations with y/our losses!
How to go to the essence of this mirage and to be released?
To be free from the Avatar holding us in duality ~ thee * me.
To see and realise the Promise I made to your Divine Goddess;
the changes to captivating Illusions darling & to wish you 'Adieu'

*

UNIVERSE IS SPACE
In*out ~ Multi * dimensional***Be here right now * free!
Still sending you light beams across the Crystal Galaxy
Star 8 * Love frequency ~
Cosmic flight through Bliss' Milky Ecstasy.
Take care ~ too much to ever understand
Unconditional LOVE Utopia ~
***

If you got through this and I hope you did then you have got the Full
lesson of our Sensitive life. It's essentially about My own 'Space trip'
finally Realising Mind-Form & being able to go to the deepest level ~
of my psyche*emotional*Attachment, my LOVE *trance, my Spiritual*
Soulmate/Avatar bond which I had with you and Releasing its illusion.
You did this when you left me & immediately transferred your feelings!
It's not to blame you, I have been holding this 'negative pain' and
I am healing it not suppressing it. I held this story for so long in me
because I still have Compassion and I never wanted to hurt/lose you.
It can be tough and you might not agree; It's a fucked up, cruel World;
My own Unconscious Ego-reflections * Is what it is * just Cosmic Space!
That's the end of my story I wish it was more wonderful but It is Magical,
* Sacred Mystery! You can forget our dream and carry on with your life
knowing the truth of us ☺I hope our Stars cross again one day ~
I send you my Love

*

<u>*Doing It in an Unconditional Love Direction ~ Not a Contradiction*</u>
White lies "Yes she's completely & deliberately avoided you ~
because she knows that you are still madly in Love with her."
'It's both a blessing and a curse to feel everything so deeply'
'Each Fragment of Life is Sacred * These are Your Children'
** Love Conscious Sensitivity ** One of my deepest lessons:

'Life is simple ~
sharing Loving Kindness
from the heart'

* x*

<u>*Hey*Cosmic*</u>
"I hope you have found a beautiful direction in your life.
Without any expectations I just wanted you to know because
I would want to know ~ that my life didn't work out ~
that my dream didn't happen.
I wanted you to know that I look back on what we had together
and I believe it was the best few years of my life.
In retrospect we always see the truth.

He never really wanted me, I was never the one for him.
I fell deeply again because that's what I do. He ended our story.
Now after a few months he is planning a life
with someone he never met. I am broken again."

"I am still at work, my best friends don't talk to me anymore.
I am alone. I have to start again. I don't know what to do. Karma I guess
for breaking your soul ~ I am sorry. I am not writing to gain sympathy or
to be forgiven or to make myself feel better or to ask anything of you.
Just to connect and tell you I will always regret how much pain I made
you feel. Sometimes it is impossible to move forward in your own life
without destroying another. I want to know you are happy x"

<u>I am your light worker help me to bring you back into the light</u>
Hallo Baby*** I hope you are jumping through the forest and running
thru the Monsoon rains, I hope you are shining again your eyes alive.
Tell me how you feel if the storm clouds become too dark and share
your spirit. Tell me how you feel when the sunbeams caress your face
tell me if you see a cosmic rainbow***:)

I want to see that smile in your face and eyes ~ I want to feel
you are happy. I am being as completely honest as I can be.
I have been deeply hurt by you I am taking a big chance in
communicating with someone who let me ~ your lover die
slowly without any remorse only cruelty. But in Your first letter
you realised that was important because you could empathise
finally with my pain because of what's now happened to you.
I am going to try and support you out of your depression ~
You're intelligent but your behavioural swings are extreme.

I have known your ups and downs over a long enough tim down too
although I have some insight but we have unique behavioural patterns.
There is Absolutely No blame if I say something you don't like please
don't take it as a negative reproach. I have read what your closest family
thinks of you and it was not the woman I knew but it was a unified view!
I fought beside you against that view, but we have to take it into account.
You have been hurt it's terrible IT was Terrible for me too, we are human
beings with deep feelings and craving mental & physical attachments
**

<u>It's never not that ~ Just Is</u>
Trance state ~ 'Life is here now * the only place it can be'
Unlicensed, no rules, more spontaneous ~ everything is Pixels.
Conditioning - "I think Artificial Intelligence has already taken over"
Subconscious dreaming * Projecting 3D fractals onto a screen
Reflecting a reality ~ Manifest your best version of Happiness

Friendship!

*Last time you reconnected with me because your life had gone to shit
and you desperately needed support, it seems this 'communication' has
now ended. From what happened to you finally you also seemed to
realize the consequences of one's actions especially to the people who
had opened up in love and trust and been betrayed. You talked about
friendship and communication and being lost. Obviously you
just needed help as you said and no one else gave a shit.
I have been in a depression for the last 18 months and I
understood deeply the loss and despair therefore I gave you
my last bit of light as obviously I didn't want you to suffer
the same negative feelings of total rejection and denial
as I had experienced from you! I was amazed how you
could reopen contact ~ only when it suited Your own grief!*

*It's not my belief to inflict pain if it can be avoided so I
came back into your negative World and gave you what you
needed from someone you could believe in. It was a big decision
on my part after the way you had treated me. I know you are smart
enough to realise this if you ever think about it. It seems from your trip
to the UK that you were smiling again and getting some love since then
you've disappeared. There is no sense in anything but what You need,
with No obligations to anyone else! And so 'It is as it is' ~
How to realise the reality of this nihilistic perception in you?*

*Fine I take full responsibility for what happens to me although ~
there are emotional catalysts. This letter is not to discuss this again
but to let you know that I feel that we have come to the end of our
journey together and that I have no more light to give you and you
certainly gave me nothing back! It is what it is ~ Now it's the end and
I am moving on with my life as I have to do under the circumstances.
I hope you are doing the same and you find what you are looking for ~*

Greedy Dreams

So now you get a feeling of what I went through the last two years. August 6th I returned to Anjuna to full stress, your negativity that I couldn't change, I'm sorry! The last 18 months I've been going through grief, depression. Why? Who really knows maybe it is all my fault! Why? My heart slowly died waiting for something, a smile, a jest. But there was absolutely no response from someone I loved and trusted. The full on betrayal, rejection, denial! The no response from the muse who said, 'in retrospect it was the best time of my life' but still had to destroy it ~ 'A Fuck you!' to my memory in order to continue in her new Egocentric-desire reflecting only her own happiness; where's Love consciousness? It was you who destroyed it and us and was the catalyst for a cruel, very painful journey for me into an emotional * spiritual dark abyss. Yes 'It is at it is' as you are finding out! How easy are those words but how difficult when it is You who has to come out of the despair of loss & nothingness. I never had any sexual relationship since; I lost the desire! Yes it takes time to come back and each one is different but as you see it's not so easy to play games with the mind. To feel like you don't exist ~ though that love of your life, who promised you Paradise and bliss with her eyes and body is sitting next to you in grim silence! But she has her heart on another vision ~ You don't fit into that dream and she's Unconscious…

'Welcome to Reality' A torture to find that someone can lie, manoeuvre behind your back without a word or honest hint to give the Love proper closure. It's selfish and each one has the right to do what we want and let's all escape in that fluffy fairy dust tale; But it's very dangerous if you lose the balance of your awareness & get lost in infatuation. You played your game it was real, but I cannot allow that light worker to upset it so I won't see him for 5 months, I'll only enjoy what gives me pleasure. Until it fucks up ~ after somehow fucking everyone off who loved you and cared. Some might call it a type of Borderline personality disorder ~ egotistical, extreme feeling of highs & lows with a lack of any remorse or empathy :)

114

A fearful questioning of one's own self Identity, I don't know! And it's not to blame anyone but to become Conscious, we're all seeking the truth of who we are but Please be kind! Then lost in Space the one she comes back to for help is the one who she helped put into deep misery but who somehow still holds up a light! Of course he would do everything to save her from going through the same Hellish ordeal even though there is real wisdom found in such suffering & this was the destiny put in front of him! How could anyone be unsympathetic to their beloved when they're hurt? But it would be easier and more sane to say, 'It is as it is' and yes to burn all memories & hopes or future expectations just as had happened to me 'I have no one, I am lost, I do not know what to do, I have no friends ~ my life is destroyed.' How would you respond? Did you even think to ask me how I felt whilst I was drowning alone ~ my heart broken as a consequence of my extreme passionate attachment with you?

So you will have to suffer I am sorry and it's better to forget me and I forget you as you are not ready for communication or for giving me anything it's only about what you want. And you have that right but when another loves you there is a conscious respect; to not get what you want by destroying another as you say but you will find this out yourself and see what it is to have a broken heart and to reflect on the truth either spiritually, astrologically, humanly or whatever it is ~

I had so much compassion that I came back to help you and give you my light. Yet you still don't know, it's not about just taking the fruit and not watering the tree. What about me the one who gave you love who you say you loved & you did! You are so afraid and guilty and negative & hurt and I feel all of that pain but I cannot be used and abused again so I want to let you go in peace while you are now around people who care for you ~ Try to understand & make a new life direction ☺

You are a super Goddess, You were my Angel of delight, my Soul mate my Sexy muse, you're very smart, true and creative and loyal; you need to believe in yourself. I thank you for all the Amazingly, Wonderful times we shared in love. I hope you recover but as it is without understanding I /we cannot move forward into a new dimension of light*life while holding onto all the negativities we still have!

*

I need to know

If I still exist in any way as 'real' in your world, some communication ~ energy, feeling would be nice or has it turned into nothing? We have had very different experiences and I can't begin to ever explain that. It will be too hard to continue for me as I went through a depression and I need to come out & find some light again! I don't want to remember you and only have pain my pain, your pain? Would you even want to see me if I came back to Anjuna? You told me to expect nothing even in our 'friendship' I can't do that anymore. I really need some communication*energy or I have to let you go forever. You let me go ~ you were never my prisoner, you are free I always respected and loved you but I can't keep you in my heart any longer ~ I have always kept you there, a beautiful memory with light shining. You came back when you needed help and even so I came to be there for you. I don't understand how you're feeling now. Yes it was wonderful times that's why I'm still in touch. You made it very clear to me that You have different priorities & we have a lot of damage too from this best time of our lives, tell me how we continue in a meaningful way or not Are you free enough this time to have a coffee with me? Tell me your truth and let us evolve together from it.

My Vision

Am I happy? Yes I am happy to be Alive and with my daughter someone giving me unconditional love. Yes I am happy to be able to see again ~ No I am not happy at all at the way you treated me like I never existed in your life, your complete denial of me as a person and rejection of all the love we shared together. Of course there was a lot of suffering for over a year as you well know. I couldn't believe that someone I loved & who said they loved me so deeply with their eyes could treat me so fucking cruelly! Finally You've somehow come to realise something of these feelings from your own experience that you wrote to me only because you needed someone to be there for you. Still 'It is as it is' ~ as you say and that is 'what you do!' Yes it is! You mention loyalty and I have been there for you, always. I'm amazed you wrote to me but that was for You something you needed to relieve something in you it was not for me. I don't believe you care if I'm really happy as in fact you haven't really communicated with me since.

You've never really bothered again I don't know why. I gave you the chance to be a friend but that's obviously not possible. I opened up again to be there for you to share something I believe in Do you know what you really want and what are you willing to share in return? It seems nothing!

I'm pissed off that I'm still writing this stuff to you again, if you want to be in touch with me do it for Me as you're feeling for me too not just because of what you need from me. Even though you said 'with no expectations' ~ but you seemed desperate and I naturally responded otherwise I would have behaved just like you which I could never do! I am tired of this, I don't know what you really want even though now you agree we did have something very magical as I have told you so many times! You destroyed it and you let me and my love slowly die alone, you never once responded to My Pain! I don't want it any more. You either make some effort to share some feeling with me or not.

20/09/2015 16:46
Thank you I am in a dark place. Life is like that.
Why are you still there after everything I have done?
How do you let go when your life is turned upside down?
Are you happy where you are?
I think about you even though I don't stay in touch.
It is hard to accept positive energy when you have nothing to return.
I am sorry for every moment I hurt you Cosmic
and I am grateful for the love you gave to me ~ Eternally
*

20/09/2015 19:00
*I wouldn't be who I am, who I aspire to be if I didn't try hard to hold up the light * It's true I was in a black hole for 18 months struggling at the deepest levels just like you are. (Time is a great healer) This sharing of Honest feelings really helps so did living with my daughter who gives me unconditional Love*Somehow I held it up and I am happy that i can still share this truth with you as I have always endeavored to do. I don't really know why I am like that ~ finding the balance between holding the light and letting go and escaping the turmoil and despair of the Mind. I have had no sexy muse lover since you but 'It is as it is ~ I have been through similar experiences before! My vision, lesson of life has been to still try to maintain something beautiful, Isn't this what a (mystical) poet does? When you go through that dark emotional valley you have to believe in something good ~ for example your children as I did with my daughter or the truths of the heart ~ trusting those moments of being in Love, being truly inspired even the truth of dealing with the pain, doubts, guilt, denial, rejection! This is the biggest of lessons, it's not TV this is REAL profound inter/human behavior and its unforeseen consequences; psychological ~ emotional, physical, spiritual! Being able to realise this makes us more Conscious of LIFE ~ You get Power to eventually come through the pain of suffering, loss, negativity, resentment, doubt, grief, fear, lonely despair I always loved the Ideal of a Romantic, sensitive, happy, Compassionate*

Bodhisattva and I am very Thankful that I have such an Inspirational ~
guide and I can freely share that with people I love and in my creations.
I am a human like everyone else but I refuse to hate which in effect only
destroys me more! I know that can be easy to say but I try for this higher
Ideal. Call it Love call it Spirit, call it obsessive, stupid even, I don't know,
I feel it gives my life meaning. That's why I am a traveller, living in Goa,
*that's why I love you the way I do. That's what fills my poems * art work.*
Ultimately You/we are dealing with a deep multi dimensional lesson, be
brave embrace it; sounds crazy but be thankful! By embracing with this
higher understanding you'll let it go ~ naturally. I've felt your open heart
& I know you have great, sincere qualities! Yes It was very hard getting
no energy back, for that reason I try to share this energy ~ with you now
but remember you have people who love you & forgive you
*and wish that you find true bliss***x.*

01/10/2015 00:39

*Hallo Baby * what I said earlier is All true but now it's finally happened to*
me. I'm feeling ill, tired, lost in a depression too. I Am empty, exhausted,
emotionally and physically. This continued - drama is ultimately My own
response to what is given to me. Your experience is not for me to Judge.
If you could send me some positive light/loving energy it would be Very
Healing revitalizing but by now I have come to expect nothing and I have
no more energy left, no more light to give! This was always my choice, I
don't regret trying to keep a Connection of light in this darkness with you
as long as I could because of who I am & the Love memories & Creative
Spirit we shared but I can only hold it up for so long alone! With so much
pain, anger, resentment, negativity existing there is a Limit to what I can
accept emotionally support & try to + lovingly transform. Of course You're
Free to live your own heart 's desires I can't Control, analyse it. You can
either feel it or you can't and you know the difference! I don't really know
the truth of what is in your life ~ of what you want to share, your visions,
hopes, your loves, dreams, even friendship? But if you feel nothing more

+ for me please tell me so I can let you/us go, renew my life & come out of this dark, broken relationship which doesn't seem (even telepathically) really to be going anywhere ~ or change it x

*

01/10/2015 16:50
I'm sorry I sent you that last message
I was bouncing through an emotional black hole*Please forgive me if I upset you and I promise it won't happen again*

*

01/10/2015 17.08
No worries. I am only worried about you.
I'll get back to you later. I'm working now

*

01/10/2015 21:56
Thank You for that x****:)

*

08/11/2015 14:37
Thank you for unfriending me. Thank you for understanding.
Thank you for showing me there is no meaning to love.
You are the only person in this world I have ever felt true happiness with.
I am sorry that the reality we live in didn't make it easy to sustain. I have passed you in Anjuna. I know you are here. I hope if we meet you will not unfriend me in reality. If it makes you feel better, Karma came right back and showed me how painful it is to be rejected by someone you devoted your soul to. I never intended to hurt you so much.
I didn't know any other way. I am sorry
*****

That's the point they don't know, nobody does
They can't KNOW ~ they're/we're Unconscious responses because of limited Mind ~ All you can do is Forgive them/us.
We are all on different Levels going through the same Maya.
Needs Understanding, Awareness, Compassion & lots of Love.

There's the Movement of Ego
There's a Tremendous need for negativity with some people!
Thinking 'I' know .... and they f....g don't Know anything!
You cannot know what's really happening!
Whatever judgment you make will be Wrong ~
but you will believe it's right from 'My' experience.

*

Then you see beyond that thinking, what Spirit is!
Happens collectively, keeps on happening ~
Who am I talking about, this Illuminati, a hated enemy?
A passionate woman, a lustful man tempted with an apple!
Lost all our innocence, animals still living in it but unknowing.
Human destiny is to rediscover our pure Cosmic Consciousness.
My Mind is continually making Mental-Formations, delusions.
Returning back to that natural state from the Mind's Ego
which got us thrown out of the Oasis of Paradise.

*

And It's Simply Amazing
Consciously looking at an ant, not as a blind-faith Personality reaction.
Affected by the word, definitions, judgment, there is no real Disorder ~
no blame game, no guilty, no more separation, there is no Perspective!
Taking your attention from the Ignorance of the Finite Thinking Mind-set.
Just being the true SPACE of things ~ coming from your Still presence.
FEELING
*

The Essential ~ Ascension
Drop every theory even *Energy*
'Borderline Personality Disorders'
Love * DMT; * Amazing that's IT!
IT'S Not Real ~ IT'S FORMLESS
You can never KNOW the Whole.
Nothing Is IT!

<u>More and more consciousness is evolving</u>
'A plant takes a while to flower
but its destiny is to flower ~'
the experience comes and goes ~ timeless…
Fighting the Central Command Ego Controller!
Just see it yourself look at the judgments you make.
S/he might be appearing as a demon or an Angel.
Looking at Life-Form as non-differential ~ neti neti.
You're reacting to the movie as if it's Real
It's Not
*

<u>Applying Limitations</u>
'God' * Divine * Space is Life can't say why ~
Stop at the Life-FORM ~ he knows he's ego!
We can come into this Evil manifestation, Lord Lucifer.
Maya in the Mind ~ Unawareness in the Mental-state.
'MIND BLOCKS OUT THE WHOLE UNIVERSE'
Acting it out as the Insane devil, fallen out of Grace.
Recognising it ~ can't make my Mind Sane
but I can take my attention away from it.
Don't take it seriously ~ no Fear
then it's Heaven.

<u>Albert Einstein</u>
"It will be possible to describe everything scientifically, but it would make
no sense; it would be without meaning, as if you described a Beethoven
symphony as a variation of wave pressure ~ Concerning matter, we have
been all wrong. What we have called matter is energy, whose vibration ~
has been so lowered to be perceptible to the senses. There is no matter"
You are a Goddess!

Anthony De Mello
"As soon as you look at the world through an ideology you are finished. No reality fits an ideology. Life is beyond that. People are always searching for a meaning to life. But life has no meaning; it cannot have meaning because meaning is a formula; meaning is something that makes sense to the mind. Every time you make sense out of reality, you bump into something that destroys the sense you made. Meaning is only found when you go beyond meaning. Life only makes sense when you perceive it as mystery & it makes no sense to the conceptualized mind."

*

She chose me
To break down in my arms ~
Seeing deep, Raw emotions * Vortices
Catharsis ~ taking out her dark Asuras
"You chose to absorb her Pain"

*

No pain; Write that down it's all forgotten!
We live a life of inhibitions, intimidations, limitation.
The only purity is breathing in the clean air ~
An overdose of LSD. gave her a glimpse of what's there.
"Really don't need acid just need to Stop my Egoic-Mind"
Discovered the greatest power within me ~ healing.
The Cosmic dance ~ once I stopped thinking.

*

Fresh Thoughtless * Realising Witness
Nothing there just I am presence ~ in your space right now.
Compassion is the Acceptance of Unconsciousness.
Compassion is Surrendering ~ it's not personal.
Your conditioned Ego state of Mind wants to REACT!
Accepting Unconsciousness ~ You have to Love your enemy.
There is No enemy you're just reacting to a concept in your Mind.
Seeing it not Mind-controlled ~ step back for a moment of Awareness.

Full Soul Therapy
Letting the darkness out ~ are we friends again?
She's gone into a deeper Level of Conscious Processing.
"It's all part of the dream, now you can awaken"
Turned out it was all an Amazing super illusion,
can't predict what's comin' next in the chaos!
'We are the dreamers'

*

Intangible Force
We are all part of the illusion*Thinking
Mental ~ 'That's It but there is no IT!'
Killed by a bee sting in Death Valley!
The enemies are created in y/our head.
Love yourself * Love your enemies ~
The Real Jihad overcoming the Ego.
The battle within not the religions outside
but Inside ~ Conscious evolution.

*

Vishnu 10
Still alive ~ Presence that you are.
The Mind can*not perceive, see it ~
Only making things up, imagine!
Feel the Silent Space ~
Who Am I? There is no I AM!
It's too busy distracted being deluded
Creating duality from the O N E N E S S.
Soul ~ 'the Mind's Creation of Separation'
You are It or you are not it * there is no IT ~
'Fanculo' an Ego state causes all the problems!
That's how it does it because of ME & MINE.

Charge*No Choice!
You suffer the consequences.
You do what you gotta do...
what's in front of you!
I gave you a deep Psychic healing
went into the night of your soul ~
Brought out your crazy demons
beyond the frontiers of your mind.
In the size of a grain of sand are
a billion different Universes.

*

You Realise
Going across an entheogenic ~ multi*Universe.
Natural experience nothing in-between.
*Surrounded by High *energy *Crystals*
Searching for the ones least Insane...
Licking her lips within Earth*ship*Space.
A very Spiritual journey ~ Visionary quests

*

Your Full Compassion in a Myth!
You saved her from flipping out
Turn on tune in ~ no more pain!
Silence in a one room Jewel box
"I could see the movie through the bars!"
"You need 5 dimensions to be in a relationship"
F R E E D * O M beyond the Mind's* veiled portal.

*

No comin' back ~ Breakdown
Not a nice feeling when you have to give your San Pedro cactus away ~
because she wants the lot! Phase conjunction * an endless crop of weed
"We're gonna take a break the cops are here." Where's the next asylum?
Remind me to read that book to the child!

Conditioning Content

Touching base eventually you will become base, grounding.
Losing False Identifications*Identifying with Mental Forms.
Id. Created with things that come into your mind ~
Feel the Space of reverence * being not making...
Then you come back into an Angel ~ 'I Am Love'
Angels can't fall in LOVE ~
Become an Angel by being Love essence.
Not outside in another, that Love is within You.
No beginning or ending
Allow the Space for it to come into this World.

*

Your Wild Nature

The Singularity has no duality ~ only here for that.
Knowing itself by looking into a Cosmic mirror ~
Just stopped thinking, experiencing for an instant.
Eternal Life in the garden of Paradise came alive!
I saw your free Conscious, no masks ~ No judging.
Screaming, speaking, soul laughing in the darkness.
Telling me that you always loved me...
Inner-Self crying in a hallucinatory cleansing!
Breaking all the chains holding y/our memories.
She fell out of her tree into psychedelic vortices,
rapids, smiling & very happy! Hyper-realism ~ Intensity
exploding inside on a forgotten, deserted Karma full Moon.
An imprisoned dragon freeing itself from deep, dark realms.
Coming to life again

*

Being Awareness * Cosmic Space

'It's not a question of being in Love with someone
It's a question of being LOVE Itself ~ '
LOVE IS INSIDE ~ EACH OF US

SUNNY JETSUN

*Inspired by the sixties Sunny started traveling the world in 1970.
His spiritual journey on the hippie trail to India took him through
San Francisco, Los Angeles, London, Amsterdam, Paris, Vancouver,
Sidney and Kathmandu to Varanasi. His arrival on the sub-continent
was the beginning of writing autobiographical verses capturing his travel
experiences, encounters with remarkable people and his quest for self-
realization; combining experimentation with drugs, sex, rock & roll ~
meditation, Love & life in general. Sunny started to open up to a multi*
dimensional Universe. He lived the mantra, "Turn on, tune in, drop out"
realising Mind's-illusions, inspired by deeper feelings of holistic nature,
empathy*energy & Space.*

*Over four decades Sunny has written & published 28 books of poetry,
created over one hundred paintings some under the name T Bird,
traveled the World and considers his masterpiece to be his daughter.
He has spent the past fifteen years in Goa, India inspired by the freedom
to experience and idealism of human consciousness.*

Sunny Jetsun books and art are available on the web at:

*Website: www.sunnyjetsun.com
Facebook: www.facebook.com/sunnyjetsun
Amazon: www.amazon.com/author/sunnyjetsun
Smashwords: www.smashwords.com/profile/view/sunnyjetsun*